CHEMO
AN UPLIFTING BREA

BY

JANE HOGGAR

ILLUSTRATIONS BY

HOLLY BISHOP

www.hollyberyl.co.uk

AUSTIN MACAULEY
PUBLISHERS LTD.

A CIP catalogue record for this title is available from the British Library.

ISBN 9781786296603 (Paperback)

ISBN 9781786296610 (Hardback)

ISBN 9781786296627 (eBook)

www.austinmacauley.com

First Published (2017)

Austin Macauley Publishers Ltd.

25 Canada Square

Canary Wharf

London

E14 5LB

Jane Hoggar via janehoggar@btinternet.com

All profits that Jane receives will be donated to cancer related charities

Disclaimer

The contents of this book are intended to be amusing but yet informative. However, they are not to be considered as a complete guide to breast cancer. The reader is encouraged to consult the websites referred to in the Glossary section and/or consult their doctor on all medical matters.

For Hannah. Gone but not forgotten.

Acknowledgments

I am grateful to family and friends who, having read my on-line blog, encouraged me to turn it into a book.

I am also grateful to Athena Bounti for her help in turning a manuscript into a book.

Contents

It's been a tough year, but I am luckier than many. I have seen grief and loss in other families, some cancer related and some tragic accidents that have turned their world upside down. I now realise that we must treasure each day and be thankful for what we have.

Do stuff.

Introduction

If you're a fellow breast cancer sufferer I hope you will find the descriptions of my experience useful. If you haven't had a cancer diagnosis then you may still find it a very informative read that will enable you to understand what happens when you are 'a chosen one' and, most importantly, you'll be more likely to notice any signs of breast cancer early enough to treat it successfully. We really need to be more aware of any little changes to our bodies and speak up in time to get a successful treatment or reassurance from the experts that your worry is not cancer after all.

I have written this book as therapy and a bit of self-indulgence although I also hope it will be helpful for other people, men and women, since I know at least one man who has had breast cancer. In the text I have changed the odd name here and there but the events really did happen as I've told them. I loved writing the experiences down and then actually reading it through to myself because it helped me to get to grips with what was happening to me. For this reason, I recommend keeping a diary if you are about to undergo treatment.

I've met people who have kept their cancer a secret and I can understand why, now that I've come through it all. After my post on Facebook that I had been diagnosed, women came to my door or sent me cards to tell me that they had 'been through breast cancer' and come out the other side. There were an extraordinary number of people I knew who had experienced a brush with 'The Big C' but kept it to themselves. Apparently there are around 200 different types of cancer, all requiring different treatments. If you don't have chemotherapy then your treatment is easier to hide and whether to talk openly about your illness, or not, is quite a personal decision but speaking about it was right for me. Telling family was the hardest part but I knew I wouldn't be able to hide it, especially when my hair fell out during chemotherapy and I was too weak to be my usual jolly self. After a few weeks of emailing and phoning my mother, brother, father, cousin and everybody in between, my daughter suggested that I started writing a blog. With her help I set up a blog that was to help me through a tough year. I began to realise that family and friends that weren't local would be able to find out all the details and situations that we were dealing with on a daily basis without having to call. It had been taking me all evening to receive calls from everyone and let them know the latest update but the blog helped them know what was going on without having to call me. This enabled them to get on with their lives over the summer while I hibernated. I didn't have visitors, as you'll read later, and I didn't always look quite as bright as the photo on the blog taken on day one of my chemotherapy.

There's no denying that chemotherapy is a challenge that takes you down to quite a low point and reassuring relatives was so exhausting that blogging helped everyone, especially me, to cope. I felt so much better knowing that my relatives were getting on with their day and not worrying that they should be helping me as I could type that I was looking rosy and feeling great while I laid in bed feeling dreadful. Fear not, pain relief is so sophisticated these days that you can blot most of the discomfort out as long as you remember to take those pills on time. Somehow, I managed to keep a sense of humour, a precious tool for managing the hideous days, as is keeping a diary or calendar to mark the days off until the treatment has ended.

I'm perking up again now and looking forward to thinking about other things, getting on with my life knowing that I've tried my best to get rid of the 'lurgy'. I seem to be lucky enough to forget pain so I can't remember the pain during the tough weeks of chemotherapy. I only remember the funny situations I found myself coping with during cancer treatment. I know my mother can hardly remember even having breast cancer which has been very frustrating when I've wanted to know details of her experience fifteen years ago. I think she has blotted it out of her memory – we're quite a positive thinking family. If anything awful or annoying happens, like falling over and breaking your toe, we are the sort that say, 'Oh well at least you didn't break your whole leg!'

If I had known that I was going to get breast cancer I would have been previously much more careful with my diet and life style choices. I've been reading a lot of stuff about diet, like people do when they have a health scare; if you're a hearty consumer of wine, chocolate, cake, butter, cream, etc., it's depressing, just to warn you.

As a result of my appointments with experts I have been convinced that lifestyle, stress, food and drink play a huge role in our chances of developing cancer. I was stressed with work and family challenges. Life threw some stress at me over the years of raising my family and I had to cope with it just like everyone else, but I think sometimes we create stressful lifestyles and pressure that could be avoided.

I had actually stopped doing any form of exercise since retiring from a dance career. Exercise, I have learnt, is thought by many experts to be important for well-being and avoiding illness. Although I thought of myself as fit, I never really worked up a sweat from sport or outdoor activities despite being a busy, active person. Swimming, running and yoga are a big part of my life now and keep my lymphatic system working after the surgery I had. Neglecting your health is thought by some to affect your chances of developing a lump. One day we will find out what causes cancer to develop but until then I am going to try and help myself avoid a recurrence. At least then I can say I tried.

I love my life, I don't want to leave yet …

🍵 Finding it

With the usual feeling of guilt, I balance the phone on the worktop amongst the empty packets of bacon as I juggle several pots and pans on the hob.

My dear Aunty Sheila has phoned and I've had to put her on loudspeaker so that I can serve up a splendid breakfast to my B and B guests who are waiting patiently in the dining room before they set off on their ramble into the Chiltern Hills with their rucksacks.

I swoop expertly past the phone,

'Ooh lovely!' I exclaim encouragingly into the receiver.

I leap back to the hob to turn the eggs over as Sheila pauses to take a drag on her cigarette,

'I know it's marvellous and Tina says they throw in cream tea for the price, now that's what I call a decent day out.'

I can just picture Sheila in her conservatory with her mug of Tetley, fag in hand, lips pursed as she fills me in on her latest holiday plans.

'Tina's perm is awful by the way,' she continues.

I snatch a glance at the clock and wonder if I'm going to get this lot served up before I have to take my son to the train station. I love the daily anecdotes from Sheila. They're all strung together with pauses for sips of tea, drags on her fag or to turn the TV down. They're the stuff that families are made of and what keep us together but there are only so many minutes in a day and her calls always seem to arrive at crucial moments. Over the years I have balanced the phone on the bath edge, the nappy bag or wherever I have happened to be as I've tried to keep up with my daily chores.

A minute later, as I've hurtled back from the dining room to the kitchen for ketchup, I suddenly remember Sheila on the chopping board and grab the phone.

She's still talking.

'My doctor says there's nothing good about a sausage-'

'Sheila!' I interrupt rather abruptly and then feel bad,

'I'm going to have to ring you back, it's mad here and I have to drive William to the station and then I'm going to the doctors with Steve.'

I hear her take a sharp intake of breath and tut.

'Well you're making a rod for your own back my girl. Make them walk to the bloody station. You were never ferried around in cars. That's why the government say children are fat now. Best thing I ever did was fail my driving test all those times. You all had bikes, that's why you've got good thighs.'

As I click the phone back onto its base and open the fridge in search of the freshly squeezed orange juice, I wonder if I've got time to change all the beds before we leave.

I stand with my hand on my forehead trying to remember what I have to do next. Did I take the ketchup through? It's usually times like this that I remember that my guests are vegetarians and I've just proudly presented them with a steaming platter of bacon.

The smoke alarm goes off sending the dog through the roof and then I remember the toast.

'Oh hell!'

I dive over to the toaster only to see one of my guests, Mrs Bradbury, standing in the doorway with an empty cafetière looking hopeful.

'Any chance of more coffee, dear?'

I'm rather miffed that Mrs Bradbury has seen me in my real light. I had been proud of my peaceful dining room each time I'd entered calmly, with my tea tray, smiling as the classical music wafted around the room.

Her lipstick is perfectly applied ready for her morning ramble in the countryside with Derek and her hair is bouffed into a classical country bob. I could always tell if my guests were having affairs. On arrival she had been over keen to tell me about her role as a Brown Owl and various other saintly occupations and she kept blushing.

'Yes of course, more coffee, I'm so sorry, I should have noticed. I'll bring it through straight away, Mrs. Bradbury.'

'And Derek wondered if you had any Earl Grey tea …' she continued,

'Oooh yes! No trouble!'

A moment later my son wanders into the kitchen,

'Need a hand, Mum?' he asks obligingly.

'Just what exactly are you doing by the way?'

He's come in to find me talking to a tea-bag.

'Thank you! thank you! thank you!' I cry, holding it up to my nostrils and inhaling deeply, recognising the distinctive aroma immediately.

I've just found an Earl Grey tea bag at the back corner of the drawer for Derek after realising we had run out and I am filled with joy. I hope it won't taste of Pledge.

'Get me a posh teapot, darling, would you?'

As I crash around the kitchen multi-tasking I have no idea that the afternoon is going to be the start of quite a rocky ride requiring much more stamina than one needs for coping with fussy bed and breakfast guests.

It's been a whirlwind year since I went to the GP that afternoon and showed him a crease on my boob. There was no lump so I wasn't worried about cancer, but thought I should mention it anyway because it looked odd. I thought maybe my boobs were just starting to go south as they do as you approach fifty.

Note to self: Always go to the GP with any unusual changes … YOU'RE NOT WASTING THEIR TIME.

Just like my friend who decided that perhaps he would call an ambulance for his chest pain and arm ache instead of going for a lie down just before having a massive heart attack. If he hadn't made the call and opened the front door for the ambulance he would be dead.

Us British, we don't want to 'put anyone out,' do we?

I had joined my husband at the doctors to keep him company on an appointment for his knee. As always we'd had a lovely chat with our GP of many years. We had said all the goodbyes and thanking him profusely as we left, I paused, remembering my boob.

'There was one other thing, I forgot all about it 'till now. I've got a strange boob.'

The doctor looked up from his computer, 'Well, I'd better have a look.'

He went over to the examination bed and started flapping about with the nylon curtain before turning to ask me to hop on the couch but I had already whipped off my top at his desk. Poor man looked rather taken aback as he walked slowly towards me, hands on hips staring at my little boob. He stepped back as though he was at an art gallery.

'Can you lift your arms up for me, Jane, and turn to the side,' he said.

'Don't like the look of that,' he said, pulling a very grim face.

'Oh right,' my heart sank, and my husband Steve immediately sat down next to me.

Some doctors aren't very good at hiding their thoughts. Ours is one of them, but he's a great bloke so we accept his direct approach knowing that he will look after us.

'I'll organise a scan for that.'

He hammered a few lines out on his computer and we all said goodbye in as chirpy voices as we could muster.

'It should be quick, Jane, you'll get a call in a week or so.'

*   *   *

I tried as best as I could to put my oncoming scan to the back of my mind as the two-week wait began.

I was very familiar with the breast unit at the hospital because I visited frequently with breast cysts which are extremely common but have to be checked in case they are cancerous lumps. Cysts show up on the ultra-sound screen as big black circles. The cysts have fluid in them and, if they are uncomfortable, they can be aspirated (drained) very simply and painlessly with a thin needle. This is why you mustn't panic if you find a lump because it is very likely to be a cyst, but you must show the doctor, just to make sure.

My mammogram at the hospital went well. It's always a tricky manoeuvre for the nurses to get your tiny tit into the clamper when you are as flat chested as me but we managed it in the end.

It must be much easier with big ones.

'Have you got it all in, Karen … or is that just the nipple, dear?'

(I made that bit up actually, they didn't really say that, but you know …)

After several different shots had been taken of my boobs at different angles the nurses came round from behind the screen.

They'd been nice and chatty throughout the mammogram, which was reassuring. It must be awful if you can hear sharp intakes of breath and tongue clicking.

'Can't see anything nasty there love. Just wait outside and we'll send you for ultrasound.'

My heart soared.

'I must be just getting a saggy boob.' I thought to myself, relieved.

*   *   *

I skipped through to the ultrasound department feeling light as a feather and after an examination with the ultrasound wand there was nothing to report and my happiness grew. The beautiful technician put the ultrasound wand down, sat back in her chair and looked at me. I was beaming.

'Why did you come in today?' she said, not wanting to let me go yet.

I was so close to putting my bra and jumper back on and scuttling out of the darkened room to freedom but I stopped what I was doing and sat down again.

'Well, it's only when I raise my arms,' I said reluctantly.

I showed her that when I raised my arms there was a crease in the lower part of my right boob. It dipped in slightly and was more noticeable when I turned to the side.

She asked me to lie down again.

She picked up the ultrasound wand. We both stared at the black shapes on the screen, not blinking until ominously a little bright green shape appeared.

'Ah!' she said quietly, 'There it is,' scrutinizing the screen while probing my boob with the wand.

She looked so sorry and kind. It must be awful having to tell people news like that every day.

* * *

My cancer was revealed, but I didn't react at all. I was probably in shock.

She took a biopsy, which was completely painless although I was a bit bruised for a few days afterwards. She numbed the area completely and then took a very sophisticated type of needle and in a split second removed some of the tissue by locating the tumour exactly on the screen. I didn't watch. I just tried to relax and look at the ceiling. I always do that for any treatments otherwise they think you don't trust them which must be most off putting. I just take a deep breath and think of all the people in much worse pain than me, easy if you watch the news ....

* * *

'We'll be in touch, Jane. Try not to worry because you've caught it earlier than a lot of people.'

I wandered down to my car in a trance. I was calm but there was a knot of fear in my belly and I could only think about my children.

Driving home was like a dream. I looked out at the world continuing around me as I crept along in the rush hour traffic, staring ahead, deep in thought. I felt a pang of jealousy as I watched some girls at the zebra crossing on their way home from school. Would I be able to laugh like that again? I couldn't imagine so but I managed a smile as they looked at me through the windscreen.

Steve, my husband, was visible through the kitchen window as he filled the kettle when I parked the car on the drive. He could tell from my expression that things weren't good and I felt mean for not letting him come with me to the hospital but I had been so upbeat when I left, insisting that it was silly for him to miss important meetings at work.

It was lovely to get home despite the news. We cuddled up on the sofa repeating the fact that I had found it early but I could tell he was petrified.

Life took over as usual during the two weeks of waiting for the results of the biopsy. This was the worst time because we didn't know how far the tumour had spread but I had lots to do on automatic pilot. I just kept busy because I knew I would be having surgery so I started the process of calling all of our Bed and Breakfast clients that were booked in over the coming months. I found them alternative accommodation, knowing that I wouldn't want to be worrying about other people. I needed to concentrate on myself now.

'I'm sorry Mrs. Patterson but we're closing over the summer due to ill health.'

Pause.

'But we always like to stay with you Jane, we really don't mind if you're a bit poorly dear,'

'No, Mrs. Patterson, we really are shut.'

Mrs Patterson was what you would call a manipulator but I wasn't having any of it this time although she tried her damned hardest to persuade me.

I could hear her striding around her stables intermittently yelling instructions to her staff as she explained her plans to me.

'It's just that my daughter Phoebe is head girl, have I mentioned that before?'

'Yes, you have,' I reassured her.

'So it's all going to be *'totes emotional'* now that she's leaving Park Lawn especially as she just happens to go out with the head boy, did I tell you, isn't that a crazy coincidence? Anyway, they have had so much responsibility this term that I wondered if they could also stay with you as a treat. I believe they turf out all the students after the graduation ceremony and so they'll have *'absolutes'* nowhere to go! Isn't that awful when you think how we pay all those fees! And, you won't believe this but we'll probably have to bring Cinnamon too!'

Cinnamon was her huge smelly dog that had spent an evening sitting between Steve and me on the sofa whilst Mrs Patterson and her husband had danced the night away with the headmaster at the Park Lawn Summer Ball. I actually felt very sorry for Cinnamon.

Knowing how drunk head boys and girls become after a whole year of being sensible I had no trouble in refusing a very disgruntled Mrs. Patterson. I had my quilt cleaning bills to think of when they didn't quite get to the bathroom on time.

It felt odd to just stop everything though. I was a hard worker and it wasn't in my nature to turn away business as I felt my whole world grinding to a halt.

*   *   *

I kept my ghastly news to myself until I could give family the full run down. Why put loved ones through the agony of waiting to know the diagnosis when it was only for a few weeks.

My daughter Holly was in the middle of writing her dissertation up at Edinburgh University and the thought of distracting her at this crucial time was too much. William, our son, was busy working hard at college so I didn't say anything to him either. Best to wait until I could tell the whole plan of action.

I started secretly making all sorts of plans for all sorts of outcomes as I pottered around the house dismantling breakfast settings and taking down notices about local restaurants and public footpaths. My thoughts had gone into overdrive and it was exhausting although sleep was impossible.

Being chirpy at home with the family is hard when you're scared.

My husband and son are quiet chaps. They prefer to listen and smile as I lead the conversations at the dinner table, sipping white wine and recounting my funny stories of the day. With my chatty daughter away at university and my new regime of no alcohol I struggled at times.

*   *   *

After an arduous two-week wait, I was seen by a registrar. I thought registrars held weddings, but I decided to trust that she knew what she was talking about especially as she had *my notes* under her arm.

Registrars, although highly qualified, often look about fifteen years old. They are very busy and vary in their ability to display their sympathy and sensitivity to your feelings.

For some reason this one sat my husband on the other side of the room as though he wasn't really part of the meeting when all I wanted to do was sit behind him with my eyes shut tight, clinging onto him as though I were about to set off on a rollercoaster at the fair.

Note to self: Move the chairs where you want them before you sit down.

I noticed that there was a breast care nurse also present so I felt that terrible news must be coming.

Breast Nurse looked concerned, holding her head on one side as she looked at me in an understanding way, probably part of her training.

'Is that expression good or bad?' I wondered, studying her face and posture too closely for clues.

The registrar was taking absolutely ages to get to the page on my notes that had the answer that we were all waiting for on it. Nursey became tired of holding her pose and kind expression and shuffled uncomfortably in her seat. We were saved when the registrar swung around on her swivelly chair like someone on Newsnight, clipboard in hand.

'The lump is really small so we have caught it early so that is good.'

'Aauurhhhhowaarrrrheheheherrrr!! Snort, sniff, sob... oh good,' I said.

*　　*　　*

The registrar didn't look up from her notes but reached for a box of tissues and passed them over without looking at me. I think she did these appointments a lot.

On hearing that the lump was small, the breast care nurse and my husband looked thrilled. They were trying not to clap their hands and high five each other. I wanted to grab them and do a 'Ring a Ring a Rosie' dance and a forward roll on the shiny green lino but I thought better of it and just wiped my nose.

Just then a surgeon came in looking tired but caring. He had a lovely smile and explained that they would remove the lump and preserve my boob.

'But I want you to take both of them off. I don't want them anymore, I'll never relax and I just want to live,' I whimpered leaning towards him almost jumping on his lap and burying my face in his armpit. I felt a song coming on, maybe something from West Side Story …

Mr. Surgeon looked really shocked. I think most people in this situation were glad that he didn't want to take their boobs off.

* * *

After explaining about the statistics of lumpectomy and mastectomy success in the whole of Europe and USA in recent years, he convinced me to let him do it his way. Apparently removing the whole breast was not necessary anymore and I had to take his word for it.

He explained that if I was really sure I wanted a mastectomy he would refer me to a psychiatrist to be sure that I wanted it done that way but that this would take time to arrange.

Of course, I just wanted the lump gone so I opted for lumpectomy thinking that I could have mastectomies later if I was still worrying constantly. You have very little time to think about what to do and this is quite stressful. I would have liked to have had a few months to research the options available to me but the thought of the tumour sitting in my breast reaching out its tentacles while the wonderful medical team waited for my decision, with all their knowledge and expertise, made me hurry up.

In the lift I squeezed Steve's hand and looked at him with relief, feeling there was light at the end of the tunnel and that I might not die after all. The other people in the lift probably thought we were having a baby or something.

We drove home feeling like some of the lead weight had been lifted. The lump was small and a treatment plan was in place.

*   *   *

Although telling loved ones about your problem is one of the worst parts of illness it was nice being able to tell the family that I was going to be fine after a spot of treatment. Bringing difficult news to loved ones is so hard but I had a full diagnosis to tell them which helped. They weren't left hanging there, waiting for results.

My Mum freaked out at first as she had had breast cancer fourteen years earlier as had my Grandmother several years before that. The good thing was that with early diagnosis, we all had the type of cancer that could be treated successfully if caught in time and I felt genuinely pleased that my cancer was at least treatable.

Mum and Granny had been cured and Granny had lived until she was eighty-one and Mum was still well at seventy-five and hurtling around Ipswich on her bicycle, fit as a fiddle. This gave me a good feeling about everything.

Owing to the fact that my mother and grandmother had had cancer, I was allowed to send my family history to the genetics centre in Oxford. I have a daughter, Holly, and wanted to know what the statistics were of her developing breast cancer. However, I was later told that Holly was only moderate risk and that neither she nor I would be offered an NHS funded test to see if we had dodgy genes and I don't mean ill-fitting trousers. I decided to leave this subject for the immediate future and concentrate on getting myself well for the time being. They said that both Holly and I would be offered enhanced monitoring in the form of earlier scans for Holly and an open door policy at the hospital for me for any worries that I may have in the future. The meeting with the genetics team was rather a disappointment. I had arrived, hoping that I would give them a sample of blood and they would tell us everything that we needed to know but it was very different. The doctor was very relaxed and explained that on the NHS we were way off the category of people entitled to a test. He explained that by the time Holly was at the age when breast cancer was likely to develop there would be new treatments available. He pointed out that as long as we were *breast aware* and reported any changes or concerns then there was no reason to intervene or perform surgery. Apparently she will be offered scanning at thirty instead of fifty.

I realise now that cancer has many forms, some more sinister than others, but early diagnosis plays a big part in the treatment success and it doesn't go away if you ignore it.

A friend of mine found a lump in her breast and after being diagnosed with the very early stages of breast cancer she told me she was going to sit her family down and tell them she had cancer. I was horrified because it hadn't spread anywhere, she was well, and they were going to remove the cancerous cells successfully so that she no longer 'had cancer'. I thought she would be causing un-necessary trauma particularly to her children but everyone deals with their diagnosis in different ways. We mustn't panic and expect the worst. It is much more useful to study our life-styles and health. If you are really frightened you will give up alcohol and processed foods and take up daily exercise. These are the things that, according to the surgeons I spoke with, statistically, will lessen your chances of developing cancer.

* * *

My research has led me to study diet and lifestyle, which has made an incredible improvement to my well-being. I'm slimmer, calmer and my face is rosier, although the latter could be the hot flushes bought on by early-ish menopause from chemotherapy. I think that hot flushes will be lovely in the winter when my husband won't let me turn the central heating up.

Cancer is the only thing that could possibly make me give up alcohol, dairy, sweets and chocolates. The difference I have felt is extraordinary and certainly outweighs the joy of comfort eating.

'Oh I could never give up my wine,' my friend Jo said, taking another deep slug of her Pinot Grigio as I poured another little cup of green tea from my jolly teapot.

'You're just not scared enough,' I replied, knowing exactly how she felt.

I knew I would have said the same thing just a few weeks before.

She leant forward on her elbows, looking at me, intrigued.

I carried on my little lecture. 'Thankfully, you don't feel the fear. I thought I could imagine what it's like to have a cancer diagnosis, but believe me you can't until it really happens. Each day feels like a gift to me now.'

It was true that everyday things like the car breaking down or the astronomical gas bill didn't bother me anymore. I just looked around me and treasured just being here.

Unfortunately, eating and drinking habits really bother people. I knew it was going to be tricky at first going out with my friends for meals, dinner parties and drinks. Some people are really offended if you don't join in when they have a drink or scoff a load of Victoria sponge and I remember that I was the same once. Before, people who couldn't eat dairy, didn't drink booze or were gluten intolerant used to really annoy me, but I realise now that they were just trying to be well and had usually had a health scare or ghastly complaint that they were trying to live with.

*　　*　　*

So, the first part of my cancer journey, as they say, was complete, finding it and seeking help.

Thank goodness for the wonderful NHS.

It is so important to detect the tumour early and I think it is a good thing that we are starting to be more aware and vocal about symptoms nationwide. I announced it on Facebook thinking that if it encouraged just one person to go and check out a worry then it was worth it.

As one doctor told me, early detection is crucial for recovery.

*　　*　　*

'I'm just having a little lump out of my boob, darling, it's really nothing to worry about but they want to be on the safe side.' I mentioned to my daughter on the phone.

*　　*　　*

I waited as my lovely Holly took in the news at the end of our daily phone call. She'd handed her dissertation in and I felt it was all right to tell her.

'Are you OK, Mum?'

'Yes! I'm only in for the day, it's fine but I didn't want you to hear from someone else and worry.'

*　　*　　*

The first thing she did, of course, was register to run in a charity race for cancer research. She raised five hundred pounds.

That's my girl!

🫖 Surgery

I spent the days leading up to my operation just tidying the house and getting a sort of recovery suite ready in my bedroom. I didn't really know what would happen and so there was no way of knowing how I would feel. I was just desperate to get on with it.

I'd closed our B&B business, as I knew this was a long-term situation and I wouldn't be able to deal with other people crashing about in my personal space. Running a Bed and Breakfast had been really fun while my daughter was away at university and her room had been empty. It had really helped financially but now we needed our house back, especially as she was graduating in a few months and would be moving home again anyway, so it wasn't too difficult for me to close. The following months were much more bearable being able to just think about myself especially as I became extremely tired. I think this fatigue came from the shock of the news and nervous exhaustion.

*   *   *

On the day of my operation we had to arrive at the hospital really early. I was so pleased that it was a day trip, it made the surgery seem really trivial like having a mole removed or something. The ward wasn't open when we arrived so we sat on chairs outside at the door. The first person to appear looked vaguely familiar and after a few minutes of chatting we realised that our children had been in the same year at school and now we were about to have the same *procedure* as my American friend put it. Not only was Gale a friend but also they put her in the bed next to me. Our rekindled friendship was clearly meant to be and we started telling each other our diagnosis stories and sent the husbands for a cup of tea but they probably had a crafty full English fry-up while us girls had to suffer *nil by mouth*.

* * *

Seeing this lovely friend in the next bed on the ward made me feel so much braver and it was nice to know that we would be able to support each other on returning home. She had the same warped sense of humour as me too so we laughed a lot.

So began an extraordinary morning that I will never forget, although my memory is rather blurred in places.

A few minutes after our arrival as we were just chatting on our beds (there were five of us all having breast surgery) a genetics specialist arrived on the ward. She visited each of the five patients in turn and also asked us all to sign a consent form. I had no idea who she was but gathered that it was something to do with our operations. Walking around the ward she would draw the nylon curtain around each bed and talk individually to us in private, giving an in-depth explanation of the science behind our impending surgery before we signed a consent form that none of us sat and read. The form was long and complicated and I knew I would need a translator if I really wanted to understand it properly. Besides, I didn't have my glasses with me, so I just scribbled my name and threw caution to the wind knowing that I had given them permission to do whatever they thought was a good idea. I had to trust them.

The lecture from the *consent form lady* is really good if:

a) You understand that sort of thing

b) You're not a trusting person like me. (I would prefer it if the doctor anaesthetised you on arrival at the hospital car park and woke you up with your coat on when it was all over and you were ready to go home.)

When it was my turn to speak with *the consent form lady,* she turned out also to be a genetics expert and I sat up and tried to look really interested, now wishing that my husband hadn't gone for a cup of tea. He's the scientist in the family and would have loved the whole discussion although he would have prolonged it into question time, which made me think perhaps that it was better that he had popped out after all. It reminded me of when I was at school and occasionally, I'd decide to make a real effort during science and try to get a good grade. I would start the lesson being really attentive but glaze over after a few minutes and start noticing things like a spider on the window or the way the teacher's nasal hair was moving up and down as they spoke. On this occasion, on my operation morning, I could just see her mouth moving around but I couldn't hear anything. I just kept nodding and smiling, wondering when I could go down to the operating theatre.

*   *   *

After she left, I sat on the bed staring wearily in front of me, still smiling from saying goodbye to *genetics consent form lady*. Suddenly Gale's head poked through the curtain like Rod Hull's Emu.

'Did you understand all that?' she quizzed,

'No! Not a word of it. Am I supposed to have learnt it all for a test?' I was getting nervous now.

'No, but I'll explain what she said. I was listening in, I hope you don't mind.'

It's good to have brainy friends. Gale is a science teacher and proceeded to tell me exactly the same as Genetics lady had, so, glazing over again, I was none the wiser and didn't really want to know anyway.

I nodded and smiled as before and soon it was over.

I was getting weary with no breakfast or drink. I just wanted to be knocked out, but no, there was lots more to do.

One of the nurses came to the door of the ward. She leant against the wall, looking at her clipboard, 'OK, ladies, put on your gowns please and then it'll be time to go down to ultrasound.'

She made it sound quite interesting as though we were on a trip to a spa or holiday resort.

We 'gowned up' and then looked at each other's back view to check that our knickers weren't on display and then set off to the ultrasound department in our slippers like a day trip from the old folks' home.

I lost Gale at this point as she was taken to another room and I sat with a lady who wanted to tell me all about her open heart surgery and then the horror stories leading up to her breast cancer operation. I was quite tired by the time I got into ultrasound. I don't actually remember it much because I was in a trance after lurching from department to department.

'Maybe now I can have my operation,' I thought, as I followed another nurse to another department, but no.

The next part was the *'Blue Dye in the Nipple'* department. This was an example of how sophisticated breast surgery is nowadays and it filled me with hope. The blue dye lights up the cancerous area during surgery apparently enabling the expert team to ensure all cancer cells are removed.

Note to self: Really must keep donating to Cancer Research.

Walking through the hospital to the nipple-zapping department in my pants and only a flimsy gown on was not pleasant. I wasn't sure if it was covering my bum and I felt like someone from *One Flew Over The Cuckoos Nest*.

There were people walking to outpatient appointments in their normal clothes with lipstick on, skirting round me in case I let out a scream or grabbed their shopping bag and ran away, laughing manically.

I felt sorry for other people in my situation who were teachers. Imagine if they saw a pupil from school.

OMG.

I then reminded myself that I had been a teacher until very recently but felt that the hospital was far enough away from my town. I was actually passed caring by then anyway. Being a teacher of drama I knew that if I saw a pupil I could distort my face slightly and pretend to be someone else with a bit of effort and imagination.

Gale has since told me that she went to visit the school that she teaches at a few weeks after her operation and one of the boys shouted across the playground,

'Hey Miss you're not dead! Brilliant!'

*　　*　　*

I sat in the waiting room for absolutely ages wondering if I would faint because I had not been allowed to eat or drink and it was now noon. I started talking to a very nervous lady who was accompanying her mother. She was so nervous that I stopped myself from blabbering on in case I was like the open-heart surgery lady I'd sat with earlier.

After half an hour a little man in a boiler suit came running along the corridor towards us carrying a rather big metal case.

'Sorry, sorry ladies! I was held up in the traffic. I have to bring this blue dye each day from another location.'

He dived into a room and slammed the door.

We all looked at each other, baffled.

Was this little man going to zap our nipples as well as collecting the dye from 'another location?'

He poked his head out of the door again.

'Jane Hoggar please,' he called.

Bloody hell, he was.

I started to feel a little concerned.

Little boiler suit man showed me onto a bed and covered me up with a sheet.

'Good day,' he said as he disappeared through another door.

It was like something from *Alice in Wonderland*. All he needed was some bunny ears. As I laid there I told myself not to panic and that even after his stressful morning in the traffic jam he had been absolutely pleasant to me throughout so I should just relax and wait for the next thing to happen, which it soon did.

A very serious lady entered and came towards me with a tray of medical bits and bobs.

'Morning,' she announced.

I think that was all she said to me for the entire treatment and I was starting to think it would be nice to have bunny boiler man back. Then, as I lay there I imagined that if she was really chatty I would be worried that she wasn't concentrating. If I was about to inject blue dye into someone's nipple I wouldn't speak. My loneliness turned to admiration. I also realised that she was probably going to miss her lunch break because we were all late because of the traffic jam that bunny boy had run into.

She injected my nipple with blue dye. It wasn't that painful and took only 0.3 of a second. I kept thinking how helpful it was going to be for my wonderful surgeon, whenever I could get to him.

I was then led through to another bed to have some photographs taken of my breast.

I returned to the waiting area and slumped into a chair wondering what I was supposed to do next and where I was meant to go, not really caring anymore because I was so tired, just in time to see another member of staff sprinting towards me down the corridor.

'Jane Hoggar?' she rasped. She looked really stressed and worried.

'Yes that's me,' I answered, wondering if I was in the wrong department and was about to have my leg amputated instead.

She grabbed my arm and started dragging me along the corridor. 'We have to get to theatre quickly. The surgeon is waiting.'

I started running too, feeling guilty for being late as though she'd caught me slipping out to do a bit of shopping before my operation. I could just picture the surgeon with all his green clothes on looking at his watch and rolling his eyes at his colleagues, cursing Jane Hoggar the shopaholic.

We ran into theatre and I collapsed on the bed. I was still panting from the running while we had a quick chat about the weather and then they gave me an injection.

'Can you count to five for me, Jane?' asked the smiley anaesthetist.

'Yes! One, t... ' I was gone.

*   *   *

When I woke up it was all quiet except for beeps.

I was in the recovery room. I swivelled my eyeballs down to the end of the bed where I could see two very voluptuous nurses on chairs examining their nails.

'Jan says there's a case of NOVA virus floatin' about apparently.'

'Oh it's dreadful innit.'

I started to feel a bit hot and panicky and they heard my breathing pattern change and immediately rushed over.

'Alright, love?'

'Not sure,' I mouthed.

They took off my oxygen mask and sat me up slightly. This felt immediately better and they called to a tiny man in green.

He had a lovely face and came up close to me,

'Relax, my dear, you are doing really well, everything is fine and we're going to take you to the ward now so that you can go home, just breath with me, in … and out.'

I calmed down within seconds hoping that the little green man could come home with me, to be there for moments like this, when the computer wouldn't work or my children didn't come home from night-time raves.

Before I left, my surgeon came to the recovery room to tell me how things had gone. I thought that was so nice of him until my brother explained that they are obliged to do that and its part of their job.

'Look, you can see your breast now, Jane,' said Mr. Surgeon. He must have been exhausted. I think he had saved many breasts in that one day.

I didn't really want to look yet but, he insisted, obviously very proud of the job. It was like being at the hairdressers when they get the mirror and show you the back of your head.

'Oh yes that's lovely,' I managed.

I was actually really impressed because there was just a line under my nipple area with a little plaster over it so I realised that after the bruising went away, the boob would look the same as before.

Genius.

Unfortunately, he explained that although they had got all the tumour out, they had found cancer cells on the very first lymph node (the sentinel node) which meant that they had had to take away the first layer of lymph nodes from my armpit for testing. Luckily these later turned out to be clear of cancer, which meant it was unlikely that the cancer had spread further. I had to wait two agonising weeks for this information mind you. This lymph node business meant that I had a drain coming from a tiny hole under a plaster in my armpit. This consisted of a thin plastic tube leading to a bottle to collect the body fluid that the lymph nodes usually deal with. I would have this contraption for five days until my body adjusted to draining fluids with fewer lymph nodes.

I was wheeled back down the corridor to the ward. Everyone passing looked down at me sympathetically, wondering what had happened to me.

'Boob job,' I wanted to say, but don't think I did, although I was still very woozy so who knows?

As we entered the ward a nurse walked passed.

'You were AGES,' she announced, looking at her watch.

'Is that good or bad?' I whispered, too woozy to care.

My husband appeared, looking drained.

It must have been so awful waiting.

I will never know why I had been ages, probably the blue dye man's traffic jam. On tired days I imagine that they had found a very tricky network of cancer cells that had taken all afternoon to remove.

I don't really remember going home.

I think I was still half anaesthetised.

*   *   *

At home I sank into bed and began the recovery with my good friends paracetamol and ibuprofen.

Initially I had lots of visits from my brilliant mates, my wonderful cousin and my darling worried Mum and Dad.

'Don't go down to the kitchen,' warned one of my friends.

'You have a kettle and an en-suite bathroom up here. Once the family see you in the kitchen they'll think that you're well enough for cooking and cleaning again,' she explained as we chomped our way through a plate of sandwiches.

I knew she was right. Good advice from a woman with four sons and a precious husband.

*   *   *

I had the drain removed a few days later at the hospital. It was painless and I was glad to get it out because it was annoying and sore and had all sorts of strange lurgies and fluid going down the tube. I suppose it's what we get rid of through our bodies normally. One of the lurgies was a long sinew of tissue that we watched over a day as it accumulated into a sort of raspberry. I was worried that it was blocking the tube and rang the support nurse at the hospital.

'Oh no that's perfectly normal, dear, nothing to worry about,' said the nurse.

'But it's got a face,' I pointed out.

Pause.

'Which medication are you on, Jane?'

Don't under-estimate the amount of water you need to drink after an operation. I was completely dehydrated and my intestines had ground to a halt. Tap water strictly every half hour and prune juice and suppositories from the chemist if necessary. This is so important but I hadn't been warned, or if I had then I had forgotten, so I felt pretty rough.

All I can say is that every member of staff that looked after me was completely committed and a credit to the NHS considering what pressure they are under.

Well done all.

First mission accomplished.

Handy tip: Get one of those stretchy sports tops instead of a bra for after surgery. This changed my life. I had spent a fortune on new bras but they all dug in at sore places and then my friend showed me her stretchy sports bra top. It moved with me and I could keep it on comfortably all the time.

Chemo, pills and strange behaviour

A few weeks after my surgery I was invited back to the hospital to speak with my surgeon. He explained that they didn't feel I needed chemotherapy and that radiotherapy would be arranged for a few months time when my scar had healed. At this point I was at the stage of deciding whether or not to opt for chemotherapy as well as radiotherapy and I found it hard to obtain enough information to enable me to make an informed decision because I'm not very good at science and I was expected to trust the surgeon's opinion. He was insisting that as he had only found cancer on one lymph node I would be fine with just radiotherapy but I wasn't convinced. One of the main issues pointed out to me regularly at my early appointments with the breast care nurse and registrar was that I would lose my hair if I opted for chemotherapy. I think that this ghastly fact was usually enough to convince patients to be relieved that they weren't having chemo and accept the arrangements. Before I was diagnosed, this was the only thing I knew about breast cancer treatment. The headscarf was the only thing you ever saw and people didn't talk about their cancer very openly in my experience so you had to only imagine what happens.

I knew that if I wanted chemotherapy it was now or never. I wanted to feel that I had done everything in my power to get rid of any remaining cancer cells that could manifest themselves and reappear later. If I had a recurrence either in my breast or elsewhere in the future I didn't want to be kicking myself wishing that I had had chemotherapy.

At this particular appointment the registrar and breast-care nurse just kept telling me that I would lose my hair during chemotherapy as if that was the deciding factor against it.

I didn't care. In the grand scheme of things, a bit of hair loss seemed trivial.

My mind was really set after a chat with a good friend of mine and I will be forever grateful to her for her advice and encouragement.

Louise used to call on her 'hands free' as she drove to visit her sister who was also fighting cancer.

'You have to have chemotherapy. You need every soldier fighting for you after this is all over.'

Those words rang in my head for days and still do.

'Yes, well... I wasn't thinking of chemo... the surgeon said I don't need it, just radiotherapy,' I stammered.

*   *   *

At the time, I didn't want to agree with her and I felt sick because, of all my friends, she was the most switched on and worldly wise on the subject and she was adamant that I should have chemotherapy. I had gladly agreed with the surgeon initially when he had advised that I would be fine with just radiotherapy. I started to ponder my situation and reassure myself that he was right despite not being given any information to back up his decision, mainly because they just don't have the time on the NHS to hold explanatory lectures for tired mums. I realised that I needed a second opinion.

I admire how my friend always asks questions and has to have things proved to her before she agrees with anything. She always remembers details of all the things happening in my life and names of people I've told her about. She has been so committed in the care of her sister, my soulmate, who we were supporting through a brain tumour, keeping in touch with the surgeons and oncologists, contacting them and demanding in-depth explanations for all of their decisions.

*   *   *

This conversation changed my whole plan, as I couldn't stop thinking about it. We booked a second opinion, privately, from another surgeon which cost one hundred and seventy five smackers. This breast cancer specialist was also really pleasant, but insisted that chemotherapy was not necessary.

Fortunately, my husband, who is an academic, went into a discussion on statistics and how they are modelled. He was quite right to get our money's worth as we'd only been in the consultation room for five minutes and I'd just been nodding and agreeing with the surgeon as usual. I was grateful to Steve for joining in.

Eventually this surgeon, after a bit more discussion, agreed that chemo wouldn't do any harm, which actually, I decided, meant that it would be a good idea. I was grateful to be given an appointment with an N.H.S. oncologist a week later.

All the people I know who have had private treatment for breast cancer have had chemotherapy which intrigues me.

'Of course you should have chemotherapy,' my oncologist chirrupped as she thumbed through my notes.

My mouth must have fallen open.

It just proved... what did it prove? I suppose it showed that every patient's diagnosis is different and you have to make sure you talk it through with as many of the medical team members as you can before you make your decision. It has to be *your* decision and I was glad to have an oncologist agreeing with me. If I hadn't had that one little sentinel node with cancer cells on it, I probably would have stuck to the non-chemo option. The specialists use statistics to form their opinions but in the end it is up to you what you choose to do because no one can give you a guaranteed prediction of what your body will do in the future. My GP recently told me that I should listen to the medical oncologist over the surgeon with regards to non-surgical cancer treatment. He said that surgeons are technical but oncologists are more systemic, meaning that they look after your whole body.

Although I am sure that the different doctors try to communicate with each other, sometimes you receive mixed messages from the different departments. This was highlighted to me a year after my operation. I had been suffering with pain in the operation site and at a visit to my oncologist she had suggested that I should have a CT scan if the pain persisted. Six months later, a registrar examined me and told me that I didn't need to go back for a further year. This was great news, but I explained that I was concerned that I still had breast pain. He dismissed my worries saying that he was not concerned that there was a problem relating to breast cancer and that I should talk to my GP.

On hearing this tale, my GP booked me a CT appointment immediately and warned me to always voice my concerns.

The clear CT result has helped me to move on and also believe that there are no remaining problems that have been missed. You must take control and persist if you are worried about anything.

Don't get annoyed when people tell you to stay positive when you tell them you've had breast cancer or are about to have chemotherapy. They mean well and can't think what else to say. I'm sure I used to say that and I suppose it's better than saying nothing. What can you say really?

'Oh shit, poor you.'

Some people said that as well …

* * *

The first part of my chemotherapy was a meeting with a cancer care nurse at the hospital. We were taken into a room used for counselling sessions and results. I wanted to cry when I went in. I think it hit home what was happening when we had special attention from the staff and I imagined all the poor families that had sat in this room to be told awful news, it sort of hung in the air. Our nurse was so lovely and explained various details of my treatment that included:

1. We had to wear condoms (guffaw guffaw). Perhaps this is something to do with the chemicals that would be dripped into my body. I never did find out the exact reason and my GP didn't know anything about it either when I asked him when my husband could stop using condoms months after the chemo treatment had finished. He looked baffled and couldn't explain why the nurse had instructed us to use them in the first place. It showed that GP's only refer you, they don't know everything about cancer treatment. Sex during chemotherapy is for superhumans anyway in my opinion so it wasn't really discussed for long.

    > Me: 'When I'm all better I can't wait to have rampant sex again!'

    > Husband: 'Ooh! Who with?'

2. I could have counselling if I wanted.

3. There would be side effects from the drugs.

4. My hair would be very likely to fall out, but I could have a free wig (guffaw guffaw).

5. I had to buy a thermometer to check my temperature throughout the chemo.

*　*　*

To go with the chemotherapy, I was given steroid tablets, anti-sickness tablets, an immune system booster injection (I did it myself, into the spare tyre every morning for the first week of each cycle, very impressive and easy) and paracetamol to take for three days after each 'infusion' - the word used by some nurses for the intravenous cocktail of drugs dripped into you during each chemo session at the hospital.

*　　*　　*

My chemotherapy drugs were called FEC.T, with each symbol representing a particular drug (see the Glossary). They were administered two months after my operation. I was given the 'FEC' part first, in three doses in three-week cycles. The 'T' part was given as the second half of the treatment, again in three doses in three week cycles. The whole thing took 18 weeks I suppose, just worked that out …!

Each visit lasts a couple of hours, longer if you opt for the cooling cap treatment, as long as you don't catch a cold or anything. If this happens they send you home and postpone your infusions which is very distressing because you really prepare yourself mentally for them.

*　　*　　*

Arriving at the hospital for chemotherapy is much nicer than going for general appointments. The chemo outpatients department is a lovely light room with smiley staff who are pleased to see you and comfy chairs that you sit in straight away. I always ended up chatting to other patients although some people preferred to shut their eyes and snooze through their whole visit. Those patients had probably heard me talking before, and knew what a motor mouth I am so pretended to be asleep.

I met so many wonderful people over those weeks during my chemotherapy appointments but had to bear in mind that some of them were struggling to stay alive. There was a wonderful old lady who, only when pushed, revealed that she had worked for Bomber Command during the war and a lovely chap who Steve could have talked to for days about Morris Oxford Woodies (whatever they are). The spirit shown by some of the people was really amazing.

*　　*　　*

I hit it off with my nurse immediately on the first day when she starting inspecting my hand looking for a good vein to put the needle in. She said what nice rings I had and I thought she'd said what nice veins I had and I went into a whole babble about how we all had fat veins in my family. She got the giggles straight away and never really stopped and of course I love it when people think I'm funny. I think I just ask questions and talk about things that people usually keep to themselves and I often get the wrong end of the stick, which is always amusing. Anyway, despite thinking I had fat veins it took two attempts to get the needle in.

During this first infusion a lovely lady volunteer came and offered to rub my feet. Of course I accepted, but felt sorry for her when my feet shot out from under my long hippy skirt. My feet are size nine and look like the Ugly Sisters' feet when they are trying to fit the glass slipper on. It took her all morning and I could see my husband looking up from his laptop wondering if she rubbed husband's feet as well but she wouldn't have had time. I never saw her again after that first visit and I suspect that she avoided visiting on the days when my name was on the list.

Steroids and things

Once the drugs had been administered from a drip fed into my arm I was sent home. The whole visit took a couple of hours. I hadn't known how the drugs were to be infused until the first trip. I had just seen so many fund-raising adverts with morbid actors in sepia films with various tubes going in at various places. These films are to persuade people to donate to research which is desperately needed, but they are hard to watch if you have just been diagnosed. For my treatment the tube just popped in the back of my hand. I had cups of tea and lunch and it was really not scary at all. There is another place for drug infusion in a larger vein near your neck. This is used for other drugs or if they can't get it in through the hand and is called a Hick line (again, see the Glossary). In my experience, there were a few failed attempts at getting the needle into my hand but there was always someone on the team who could do it eventually.

Sometimes a bit of blood escapes and you get some localised bruising but it doesn't hurt really.

When it was time to leave I was given the huge bag of tablets mentioned earlier and sent on my way. Its a good idea to make sure a nurse goes through the list with you and makes sure you have good instructions for when you administer your drugs at home.

There is a lot to remember. Writing it down helps.

* * *

So, after my first infusion of drugs, the FEC part, I went home to bed, relieved that the first hurdle was over. I was fine for a while, but then threw up quite dramatically a few hours afterwards. I decided that the bottle of fizzy water in the car on the way home was something to do with it. This scared me of course because I wondered if every day was going to be like that, but that was the only time I was sick throughout the whole treatment. My oncologist gave me some stronger anti-sickness drugs to stop it happening again. Unfortunately anti-sickness drugs make you constipated, which, when you are trying to pass poison through your system, is not good. Get some glycerin suppositories ready for each afternoon. I didn't think oral laxatives would be very nice on the stomach so went in at the other end! Let me tell you I felt so much better after a few visits to the loo and I'm sure I coped better and didn't feel sick because my system was regular. You can get these little torpedo glycerine suppository capsules over the counter in the chemist and it gives you something to do in the afternoons while you watch *Flog It!*

The drugs are given every three weeks and the following is the general pattern that formed for me anyway.

Week one: I felt sleepy and I had a very active digestive system. The medication gave me shocking, musical flatulence. Don't go out in public if you are having trouble with your bowels, a common symptom during chemotherapy. My friend rang and asked me if I wanted to join her at Ascot in *The Royal Enclosure* to cheer me up. Very kind, but bad timing – so I turned that one down. Can you imagine? Even horses don't fart that loudly and I would definitely have done so if I had curtseyed to the Queen. Even the word enclosure made me nervous. The thought of being trapped in a small space with hot flushes, flatulence and the Queen was too much to contemplate. Added to that, the nurse had warned me to stay away from stuffy public places if I wanted to avoid catching colds and being sent home on infusion day with a high temperature. She advised me not to shake hands with people and one cannot refuse to shake hands with the Queen and I'm sure she catches colds like anyone else. I bet she gets some real stinkers with all her worldwide hand-shaking. Maybe that's why she often wears gloves, I would.

Flatulence really kept our spirits up as it is one of our family's favourite subjects, well my husband's anyway. I used the new found skill to diffuse any family disagreements. Heated discussions about our new arrangements for domestic chores would be diffused by a low toned trumpet sound. It would last for many seconds, especially funny if I managed to keep a straight face throughout the performance as I sat in my comfy chair in the corner of the kitchen like an old granny.

Week two: Sleepy and, if you don't eat chicken livers, onions and spinach by the bowlful, lightheaded because your blood count is at it's very lowest. Try and plan your diet carefully and eat iron rich foods so that your blood test results are good the day before your next chemotherapy shot. The hospital always check your iron levels before they give you your infusion to make sure you are strong enough to cope.

I was in the middle of week two during my daughter's graduation ceremony that was being held in Edinburgh. I had to miss the trip because I was too weak and would have caught too many germs on the journey there or in the stiflingly hot hall. My son rigged up the web-cam for me. Not only did he stay at home with me, he even worked out how to take a photograph of it on the computer. We had a very emotional moment together when Holly looked up at the camera and shouted,

'Hi, Mum!' as she walked back from receiving her scroll. We could also see her proud dad beaming in the audience. Modern technology continues to amaze me in every area of life.

Week three: Feeling fine and getting back to normal. Annoyingly bouncy and jolly actually until they give you another shot and you feel shit again.

*   *   *

The other challenge that I had was adjusting to the effects of steroids. Steroids affect people in different ways. For me I felt pumped up with adrenalin so I was up making pots of herb tea and looking at Facebook at all hours of the night. I would then go back to bed to sleep deeply with very vivid, strange dreams about people from my past in big hats speaking in loud voices. Fortunately you only have to take the steroids for the first three days after each infusion so it wasn't for long.

Once, after a night of reading magazines with the dog while

everyone slept soundly, I staggered back to bed at 5 a.m. to collapse into a deep sleep.

The eight o'clock bus to Aylesbury thundered past our bedroom window later, waking me from a dream. I had been saving a baby seal from the pond at the park opposite our house. I awoke, exhausted as I lay in a stupor for a few minutes just remembering who I was. I lifted my head from the pillow to see that I was lying in a Superman position with my foot on my knee and my arm over my head, fists clenched. My husband was coiled up in the corner of the bed with his cheek nestled against my fist. I hoped I hadn't punched him. Must watch that eye through the morning.

I quickly resumed my Sleeping Beauty position and pulled on my groovy turban that I'd bought in advance ready for being bald, just as Steve woke up. I loved my stretchy turban. I liked to think of myself as one of those retired actresses with deep red lipstick and a cigarette holder on a chaise longue.

When my daughter moved home after graduating from university, she announced that she would like her new bedroom theme to be 'Surfer Beach Style.'

I told Steve that evening about her decor plans and asked him if we could have a new theme to our bedroom. Looking around the room, taking in the table of drugs and syringes, moving over to where I was sprawled on the bed in my leopard print turban and red satin dressing gown, he proposed 'Transvestite Drug Dealers?'

The Half Way Mark

When I finished the 'FEC' part of the treatment I felt really lifted because I was 'half way there.'

Now for the 'T' bit. Taxotere.

One morning I was sitting at my dressing table, unable to find my glasses, squinting at a tiny bottle of eye drops and wondering if they were the ones from the vets we'd had for the dog last year. My eyes were sore and dry, one of the symptoms, and I needed relief instantly. The penny didn't even drop when I managed to read, 'remove contact lenses.' I knew Gnasher had bad eyesight towards the end, but I didn't remember taking him to Specsavers.

I also had itchy spots, like gnat bites all over me and I was quite relieved to realise it's one of the side effects of Taxotere. I'd thought we had a bed bug, but only on my side of the bed. This got quite virulent over the weeks but I found that Sudocreme worked wonders and I knew it would stop at the end of the treatment so I didn't panic. Interestingly, my friend who was having her chemotherapy privately was given a biopsy of her spots at great expense.

*   *   *

I was quite blasé about the whole chemo thing by half way and wasn't really bothered about the 'T' bit. It was quite a disappointment therefore, when I felt really ill after the first infusion. I kept reminding myself that the oncologist had said that the discomfort would lift after around five days. I had a rash of itchy spots on my front and back and a terribly upset belly … won't go on about farts yet again, but it was not pleasant. My organs and bones really hurt, too, and I wondered how on earth people managed to go to work like this …

On day six of the Taxotere I got up and forced myself to do some yoga and sit at the computer and I did feel better than if I had stared at the TV in bed. I think moving around keeps the blood flowing through the veins and can only be good even if you collapse back into bed after a while …

I didn't want to write this book unless I could think of nice things to say rather than, 'Oh heeeelp me. I'm melting … never have chemotherapy whatever you dooo …' because chemotherapy is great for getting rid of cancer. Don't give up, it's worth it.

A wonderful nurse told me off for not taking my painkillers at precise times throughout the tough days. She explained that I should draw up a timetable and take the paracetamol and ibuprofen exactly on time before I was even in any discomfort so as to keep ahead of the pain. This worked a treat when I realised that I had been waiting until I was hurting before I took a tablet. Take paracetomol and then ibuprofen in between the paracetomol doses but check with your G.P first on the exact dosage for you.

I knew my oncologist would ask me if I would like to lower the dose of Taxotere if I was really struggling … I really didn't want to do this as I felt that it wouldn't be a proper treatment. I was hoping that there was a drug that I hadn't been told about yet, that knocked you out for five days until the painful week was all over but, alas, there wasn't one. I tried codeine but it made me hallucinate and stop pooing. This last side effect was great for the rest of the family as the farting novelty had worn off and they were just walking calmly around the house with pegs on their noses but I worried that it was all gathering up inside me to later cause a catastrophe. I'd heard that some other people didn't get on with codeine either.

Basically, 'week one' of Taxotere can be very tough for some people so get your timetable and pills ready so that on the first morning of week two you will hopefully start to feel any pain slowly subside, day by day and remember that week three is 'perking up week' and not far away.

By the last week of the whole treatment I have to admit I was a mess. My eyes were red and streaming due to having no eyelashes and I had burnt my face during a ten-minute chat in the sunshine with no sun block on. That made me look about a hundred years old. I was not happy and felt stupid and annoyed that I had let it happen. Your cells are not renewing themselves as normal so the sun is lethal. I didn't know I was so vulnerable and was upset that I hadn't been warned more of the dangers of sun exposure even in small amounts.

Emotional

I had been crying at silly little things which is rather a family trait anyway. I always sit at the back at school concerts because I sob so much, even at other peoples children as well as my own. There was one incident, years ago, when I realised I was weeping at one of my children's friends as he played the violin beautifully at a school concert only to notice his mother secretly check a phone message during his performance and that made me cry even more. Anyway, I started to wonder, after crying quite dramatically at an episode of *60 Minute Makeover*, if perhaps this crying was out of control because of the drugs or just the exhaustion of coping. My friend Vanessa had advised me to let my feelings out during my chemotherapy and not to bottle them up because it was bad for the recovery process.

'If you need to cry then go with it and let it out darling.'

On my way home I wondered if she meant cry in public or just quietly in my room … I mean you never know when it's going to hit you really. It's half acceptable in the kitchen at home but not half way through the checkout in Waitrose, everyone would immediately assume you were mad and move to a different queue. I decided to consider crying next time the feeling hit me instead of humming and changing my thoughts to other things.

This happened one afternoon, fortunately at home. I had made the mistake of watching the ghastly lunchtime news as I sipped my Miso soup in bed. Tears were trickling down my cheeks and instead of wiping my nose and letting the feeling pass, returning to my book or calling my mother for a natter, I let the tears continue and it felt fantastic. I was crying for myself and for all the courage that I had mustered to weather this nightmare. I was just feeling a great weight from somewhere deep in my chest working its way out when I heard my husband charging up the stairs. My face had crumpled into a distorted mess and I was enjoying it, but I froze. Should I carry on sobbing in front of Steve?

'Darling it's alright,' Steve rushed over, looking worried.

My face didn't know whether to carry on enjoying the blubbing or stop here and now. I found a smile and the crying stopped because I didn't want to upset Steve. Looking back now I think that it is really important to cry and get that pent up emotion out at some point, which is probably what shrinks get their patients to do isn't it? I decided to try my next crying session at a poor unsuspecting reflexology or shiatsu massage appointment and a few months later my friend recommended that I took advantage of the complimentary therapies offered to cancer patients at our local hospice. When I called them I was put through to a lovely lady called Jenny who listened to my story and when I started sobbing on the phone she gently suggested that I visit her for a chat about my emotional baggage (my words not hers!) She said that I needed to get all the pent up anxiety out if I wanted to move on so that's what we will try and do. I'm so glad I rang because I nearly didn't, not wanting to take therapy time away from people struggling with further advanced cancer, but Jenny explained that that was what they were there for and that they had time for everybody.

Visitors

The most difficult part of this treatment has been refusing visits from wonderful friends because they are so kind and we love each other so much.

The nurse had said that the people who coped best with chemotherapy were the ones that kept a low profile and had phone calls instead of visits to avoid catching colds from hugs and kisses. I always hug and kiss my friends, but she said that they wouldn't always know if they had caught a cold and if it was passed onto me I would run the risk of chest infections and hospital admissions so I should put myself first and hope that they would forgive me. Most of them did, but I am dreading my phone bill.

*　　*　　*

Try and have cancer in the summer because it must be much harder in the fluey British winter!

*　　*　　*

Whenever you have chemotherapy, your day to day events continue and the family still have to get to school and to work. Keeping life as normal as possible is comforting throughout the chemo time. Whatever your children's age, if you have a family, they still need to keep up their social life, hobbies and commitments and I certainly found it a joy when my son would unicycle past me followed by the dogs chasing behind down the hall on his way to the park. Just make sure everyone uses the hand steriliser in the hallway, or washes their hands when they come in.

Your friends will be only too pleased to help you if you ask them. When someone says,

'If there is anything I can do, let me know,' take them up on it straight away.

🫖 Wigs Hats and Baldness

We booked an appointment at the hospital Wig Fitting department.

'The poster looks rather old fashioned, I wouldn't get your hopes up,' pointed out my husband as he perused the notice board in the waiting room.

'Oh it'll be fine, I'm quite looking forward to it,' I retorted, looking across at the poster of a 1960's false head in a blue rinse. Woolworths window display model sprang to mind.

After my initial consultation with a cancer care nurse we had been invited to visit the wig lady after an explanation about the inevitable hair loss. The nurse had also showed us some head gear called a cooling cap. The cooling cap is a frozen helmet that you put on your head for two hours after your chemotherapy infusion. It's not compulsory but the process of freezing your scalp is known to help prevent hair loss during chemotherapy. I was considering this option until the nurse explained the length of time it took after each chemotherapy infusion, a couple of hours. I didn't sign up as I knew that I would just want to get home as soon as possible from each appointment. Also, I had discreetly glanced at people in cooling caps in the cancer treatment rooms and they had looked cross-eyed and in dreadful agony so it really wasn't for me, being of the low pain threshold type.

I can understand people giving it a try, especially ladies with beautiful shocks of auburn locks tumbling down their backs. It would be heart breaking to lose hair like that especially if you were planning on continuing to go into work as normal.

I had recently been to the hairdressers to have my hair cut really short. This was not upsetting as I often wear my hair short, but it had grown very long over the previous few months so it was quite a dramatic change. People told me that I looked younger with short hair.

Note to self: Have short hair now and forever more.

I had trouble explaining the reason for my trip to the hairdressers to my husband. He couldn't understand why I was spending thirty quid on a haircut when it was going to fall out soon anyway. Sometimes he is just too practical.

My hairdresser was so sweet and kind as I explained my plans and we will tease Steve forever about his money saving point.

As the dates for my chemo treatment came nearer, I became rather curious to know what I would look like bald.

'Would I be a Sinead O' Connor or Kojak?'

Probably the latter.

*   *   *

Whilst making my decisions about hair I had looked around at what headgear people were wearing during their chemo treatment at the hospital and it varied from:

1. A Heidi headscarf that looked like you were going to a beer festival in Austria and showed all the bald area at the back.

2. A silk scarf with trailing bow at the side, which was alright if you didn't mind people looking at you thinking, 'Oh look, she's having chemotherapy poor cow.'

3. A wig. Your friends will know but they know anyway and Joe Public won't bat an eyelid, which is good in the queue at NatWest or wherever. And little children don't ask their

mummies very loudly why that lady has no hair. I know I would ask my mummy that very loudly if I was four.

4. A skiing hat with bells on it, what the hell.

5. A bald head. What the hell.

6. A stretchy turban cap. Pretty obvious that you have no hair but I decided it would be good to have a few in the drawer for emergencies. If I didn't get a wig in time for the bald moment I would need something. I had looked in the under-stairs cupboard at home and only found my husband's beret from France, my daughter's turquoise balaclava and various woolly hats but it was going to be hot weather. The only people who wear woolly hats in summer are usually alcoholics in the park or eccentric teenagers and I hoped that I wasn't in either category.

(From top left, clockwise)

1. The Dora in Dark Chocolate.
2. Walking in public (had to whip the wig off because it was so hot.)
3. Totally bald.
4. Regrowth.

I'm only putting the pictures of my head hair in the book. Sorry but there will be no photos of my missing pubes.

*   *   *

So I ordered a couple of silky turbans online and they proved to be comfy and nondescript. Remember that your family may be finding it all harder than they are letting on, so walking around showing off your bald head might be upsetting for them even if you're coping very well with it. My turbans also kept my head warm, it's surprising how chilly baldness can be.

Wig fitting Day

On entering the wig-fitting room, Glenda the wig lady stepped out of a cupboard and made me jump. It was a small, stiflingly hot room and I grabbed a chair and sat down pulling my husband with me. We sat facing a mirror looking back at each other which made us laugh immediately. It was not the sort of outing we were used to and all these appointments and meetings had happened so suddenly. With cancer treatment there is no time to mull over your plans, you just leap into action, learning as you go along. So there we were feeling out of our comfort zone and rather tired.

Glenda paused and gazed at my frazzled face for a few embarrassing seconds. I started to speak although I hadn't thought what to say yet, as usual, but she stopped me with a held up hand,

'You are *The Dora, in dark chocolate*. Fabulous!'

She spun round to face the cupboard door.

'Pam, get me a Dora in dark chocolate pronto would you darling?'

My God there was another woman in there.

Lots of rustling of plastic bags and then a high-pitched squeak,

'No dark chocolate, only pecan, Glenda.'

Glenda looked over at me with a frown,

'How would you feel about a colour change Jane?'

'Well, whatever you think really,' I said.

NOT A GOOD THING TO SAY, it gave her a free reign.

Here I was again, agreeing with everyone.

'Well let's try you for size, we can always get the dark choc in later.'

She whipped a wig out of a plastic bag and we started wrestling it onto my head.

When the scuffle finished and I was sweating like a pig I threw my head up and looked at my husband in the mirror.

It was useless.

We both collapsed in hysterics because I looked like someone off Corrie in the 60's. All I needed was a fag and a pair of Marigolds.

Glenda was deeply offended. And she came over with a brush and bouffed me up.

This looked even funnier and The Dora in pecan was sent back to the 'voice in the cupboard.'

*   *   *

We tried many more; the Textured Pixie in Mocha, The Crowd Pleaser in Voltage Rouge, The Glam Slam in Risky Red.

The names are what set us off, but after a while we were just exhausted from laughing. It was that sort of laughing in assembly at school that is more like crying because you're not supposed to and Glenda was not happy, which made me feel awful because she was such a kind lady.

Eventually we found a sort of trendy bob style called The Denise in Mahogany that instantly looked normal in a Bobby Crush sort of way (young people look at Bobby Crush online). I looked forward to smiling and winking at everyone in it. Maybe I could take up my piano lessons again and Glenda said she would order it, probably glad to get rid of us.

She also said that it suited me because I had a really long face. I took that as a huge compliment.

We left feeling tired and hot but glad we had made an effort.

The daft thing was that two weeks later, when I was completely bald, we were called in again to be told that there was no Bobby Crush wig after all as it was out of stock and they had chosen something completely different for me and that was that. Damn I'd been practicing my scales and the whole wig fitting performance had been a waste of time. Nevermind, the laughing was good therapy so I gratefully bought the Tori in Chocolate home with me and hung it on a bottle on my dressing table. My lovely friend in the salon next door to my house trimmed the fringe for me, which improved it a bit, but I knew it was just going to take a while to get used to it.

*   *   *

A few weeks later I ordered a couple of wigs online because Tori and I weren't getting on brilliantly. The new wigs were gorgeous but obviously expensive so if you are wig hunting, start early and take your time. If you're offered a free wig on the National Health (actually I think mine was offered by a hospital charity scheme) you need to make sure you try on lots, which may mean going back a few times if they are out of stock, etc. Go before you start the chemotherapy because on my second visit there was a lady in the room with us with a terrible cold. I donated my three wigs to new patients when I finished the treatment. Your local hospice will accept them gratefully. Don't despair if you have a dodgy start, get your wig early and start wearing it to get used to it. And remember, it's only for a few months because when you stop taking the drug your hair will start to grow again.

Don't let your kids wear your wig to the pub, it will cause

pandemonium, especially if your son is the same height and spitting image of you, people get confused. Also, I don't recommend wearing it in bed because it doesn't look too good in the morning.

Handy tip: My wig was giving me a headache until I realised it was actually the stretchy, netting thing that you put on before the wig goes on to stop it from slipping. I stopped putting that bit on and the headaches went away and my wig didn't slip.

*   *   *

The day that my hair started to come out was two weeks after the first 'infusion' of drugs. I was pottering around the bedroom actually wondering when it might happen. A sort of morbid curiosity. I ran my fingers through my hair at the back and, blow me down, a handful came out. I wasn't at all shocked, in fact I was rather glad to get on with this part.

I called my husband to tell him but he didn't like it and looked worried. I started pulling it out and watching it float down to the waste paper basket.

'Stop! I can't bear it, come in the garden, lets shave your head,' he begged.

'Excellent,' I was thrilled.

We bunged up my son William's very posh electric shaver and Steve had to spend the afternoon un-fluffing it but it was worth it.

I looked like a big naughty pixie.

I didn't walk around bald because I didn't want to shock the family so the stretchy turbans were great. The wigs hadn't arrived at that stage so, another reason to get them early. You have to consider that the family might be finding it all harder than they're letting on. Fortunately I was feeling quite chirpy so everyone else started to relax. We had all been wondering how I would feel once the drugs went in, as you never really know. One day at a time is a good mantra because everyone is different.

Pubes

(Don't read this if you're easily offended by talk about private parts)

I was in the shower one morning singing away, feeling that this whole chemo thing was a doddle when, on glancing down at the plug I noticed a small creature trying to escape down the plughole. I continued to sing and scrub while thinking through what I had seen, trying to ignore it when gradually it dawned on me that the creature was of the minge variety. OMG I was silky smooth. But I didn't want to look, I hadn't seen it for nearly forty years.

I lifted poor Harry hedgehog out of the plug and put him in the bin. Didn't want to scare the next person that had a shower, did I? Glad he hadn't escaped half way down the pipes, how would you explain that to a plumber?

On stepping out of the shower, I strolled casually across the bedroom, throwing my towel on the floor and going into the Lotus position for my ten minutes of quiet morning yoga on the mat. Yoga was really helping me feel good and balancing my wobbly karma and helping my numb armpit to keep mobile after the lymph node removal. Velma, our little pug dog came to sit by the yoga mat in her usual position but froze and dashed out of the room.

'What's wrong Velma darling? Come on!' I called.

I could see her eyes shining at me from the landing. She was not taking part in the yoga today for some reason. Shame, she usually enjoyed yoga. It was quite encouraging to have her company but I resumed my Lotus position.

Well, I have to say it took a lot of Karma to cope with the view as I looked down. Being a mother of two, my bald Lady Garden was a different sight after so many years in hiding.

I thought it was going to speak to me, maybe do the counting for the yoga like an instructor.

'Well hello there Jane, and relax, and one, breath in, and out, two, very good.'

It reminded me of the plant on *Little Shop of Horrors*! yelling 'FEED ME SEYMOUR!'

*   *   *

Flicking on the TV, I abandoned the yoga and hopped into bed just in time for Steve, my husband, to arrive with a tea tray. He was all smart in his suit and ready to go to work, so it was good timing. I thought how the sight of 'The lotus position' might have stayed with him all day throughout his meetings and lectures at college, poor man. He passed me a cup of tea.

'I've put the bins out, fed and walked the dog, made sandwiches and I'll ring you through the day. Here are your tablets, take them now please so I know you've had them.'

I reached for the tablets.

'Yes Sir, I mean, Darling,'

He didn't laugh so I reached my arms out and snuggled further into the duvet.

'Kiss me, darling.'

He looked at his watch and planted a little kiss on my lips. He was coping so well with the multi-tasking but I was worried about him worrying about me. He's a man of few words at times and a lot of guessing on my part has to take place. I had to remember that he had huge responsibilities at work as well as looking after me.

'Don't worry about me because I have loads of people around to call if I need help. I love you.'

'Love you too.'

Velma sloped back into the bedroom and hopped cautiously into her little bed by the window, peeping at me and probably wondering where my hair was and why I wasn't getting out of bed for her usual jaunt around the park.

*   *   *

'There is one thing I need you to do,' Steve had returned.

'Ooh yes what's that?'

'Just wake William and make sure he doesn't miss the bus to college.'

I blew a kiss,

'No problem, sweetie, consider it done.'

After watching the weather forecast for the fourth time I realised that I hadn't heard William slamming the door and running down the driveway to the bus stop.

'Hey ho! I'd better go and investigate,' I thought as I heaved myself out of bed and steadied myself by the bookcase. I was feeling groggy and as I stood up I felt my belly, full of steroids and drugs, gurgling and rearranging its contents.

'Come on, old girl, you can do it,' I muttered as my head reeled.

Velma thought I was talking to her and came to stand by my feet, loyal as always.

As we approached William's room I could see it was still dark and there were no tell tale sounds of showers running or cereal being poured.

'Willy, darling …'

Silence.

*   *   *

Our house is very old and William's room is in a hayloft that has two steps up to a small door that you have to stoop into. I sat on the ledge and swung my legs round until my bare feet sank into a cold pizza that was in a box on the floor on the other side.

'Morning, Willy, time to get up, you'll miss the bus, darling, Dad's left you a sandwich and some bus fare,' I whispered in my feeble voice. I'm such a wimp when it comes to instructing people.

I imagined how some mothers would never have tolerated this one-sided conversation. I knew I should be yelling, 'Get your arse out of bed! How many times do I have to tell you, you'll miss your bus?'

I sat on the bed, knocking over a guitar and sending it twanging across the floor.

As my eyes adjusted to the dark I could see a mop of beautiful blonde hair on the pillow and realised that William's girlfriend was snoozing next to him.

'Right well I'll be off back to bed now, but don't miss your bus,' I whispered.

I collided into the drum-kit on my way out sending cymbals crashing and as I cocked my leg over the hayloft steps a loud chemo fart escaped to announce that I was leaving, clearly stating what I thought of the situation.

Understandably they pretended to be asleep but a few minutes later I heard the slam of the door and the clomping of Doc Martins on the drive.

Handy tips for getting through chemo

With a runny nose, puffy eyes, bald head, farting like a trouper I looked across at my husband wondering if there was any chance that he still found me attractive…

This is my survival kit. Hope it helps you.

Suppositories and digestion

(Sorry, I know this is not a nice one to start with but it just sprang to mind first!!) Suppositories from the chemist are great for ridding yourself of the chemically horrible poos one experiences after each infusion of drugs. I didn't know suppositories could be bought from a regular chemist and they changed my life. This should stop you from feeling ill. The anti-sickness drugs make you constipated and it can be really painful. You need to get that stuff out of your system. Nice lemon and mint squash from the health shop was wonderful, although now I hate it! Probably reminds me of the chemo time. Alternatively, Waitrose have a lovely Elderflower variety. I got used to drinking loads of tap water, but a glass of squash was nice now and then. I gave up tea apart from herb tea and green tea. Herb tea needs to be experimented with, don't expect it to taste anything like builder's tea, but find one that you like and use a bit of honey and fresh lemon at first. Green tea gives you a bit of a lift and is meant to kill cancer cells according to some health freaks but don't have it too strong. The Chinese make it weak in a pot and I prefer it that way as it's really rehydrating. If you have wild mint in the garden, cram it into a teapot with a bit of honey and lemon.

Always have a jug of water and a glass by the bed. Don't go through the night without drinking water. You will be very dehydrated at times and it's important to drink so that you don't get an infection.

If you feel nauseous, drink a pint of water slowly over an hour and then repeat. You need to be peeing as much as you can to get the waste products through your system.

Stretchy hat

In the seventies, my grandmother used to wear a funky towelling turban when Grandad took her for a spin in their little blue sports car. We used to take it in turns to squash in the back and join them. It was rather embarrassing as they played Max Bygraves tunes really loudly and there was the turban that came out of the glove compartment as we set off, to protect her 'wash and set.' I never thought I would ever wear one but I loved mine when I went bald. I even bought one in leopard print. Wigs are alright for going out as you'll have read earlier, but at home it's really comfy to just pull on a cool turban. A stretchy turban is available online. I went on Amazon.

Chemo Food

Keep bags of dried fruit and nuts for in between meals so you don't feel sick.

If you can bear it, eat chicken livers and dark green veg because it will keep your iron levels up especially during week two when your blood count is at its lowest. Your next treatment can be postponed if your blood count is low, which will prolong the whole ordeal. A day or so before your infusion you have to pop into your GP and give them a small sample of blood which they send to the hospital for testing before you arrive on infusion day to reassure them that you will cope with the next dose. I don't know how vegans cope during chemotherapy because I could feel the liver permeating all my credentials as I ate it.

If you feel light-headed and 'headachey' then the chances are that you need some iron.

If you don't hate it, Marmite, as a drink or on toast, can boost you so much and there are good minerals and nutritious things in it to keep you well.

Similarly, Miso soup is very good for you and can make you feel better.

DVDs and photos

DVDs to watch on 'bad days', but not sad ones … you will cry like a baby. I cried at 60 minute makeover on TV … the reveal with Clare Sweeney … it was amazing …

I ordered a load of costume drama DVDs, but then my friend Mary gave me a box from her house. They varied from romantic comedies to action and horror films that I wouldn't normally watch. One morning I put on a jolly looking film about the life of Liberace. My husband came in to kiss me goodbye on his way to work just as Michael Douglas had started humping Matt Damon. It was only nine o' clock in the morning.

'Enjoy your day, darling.'

Something else I enjoyed was sorting through the photos from the loft on days when I felt reasonably OK. It was something I could leave out and go back to when I felt OK. Something I hadn't had time to do before. I cleared the loft out as well and it gave me so many things to think about and the feeling of clearing out and moving on was good too. It's really a great time to get your husband to do DIY jobs for you because he feels sorry for you. Get in there while you can.

Alcohol sterilising pump (hand sanitiser)

I kept one of these by the door for visitors to rub into their hands. I bought it online. I didn't encourage visitors, but my kids and husband used this when they came in and out to avoid spreading colds, etc. It was hard to keep reminding them to wash their hands. As the weeks passed we became a bit lazy about it but a cold can really set you back. More tricky during winter with flu, etc.

Internet

You might not like those round robins that people send at Christmas, but this is what started my idea of a blog, and then this book. I think that family who aren't local really appreciate hearing a run down of your treatment every now and then. If you don't, you will only have to explain it individually each time they all ring up and that is very tiring. It will also help them to get on with their lives if they know you are OK with a little email. People didn't like to phone me up in case they woke me.

I spent a lot of my time at the computer writing this book during my chemotherapy. If you're not going to work or keeping a job going from home, try and find some hobbies to keep you busy. If you haven't learnt to use a computer yet then maybe this is the time to do it. Daytime TV can really 'do your head in.' although I am now an antiques expert from the endless programmes I gazed at over the summer.

Write if you feel the urge, like me, you might not be able to stop. You'll never get this much time to yourself again. A medical daily diary is useful, too.

Keep a folder for all the paper work and appointments that you have. It gets hard to keep up with all the appointments and a calendar or diary is essential.

Do an Internet shop for food every so often. Your family will be doing much of the shopping and cooking for you, hopefully, so they will thank you if you have ordered in all the heavy and bulky stuff like bog rolls, etc.

Pain killers

Balance your painkillers with military precision during the tough weeks. This was brilliant advice from a Macmillan nurse. When you get home from your 'infusion,' as long as you have discussed it with your doctor, take paracetamol and ibuprofen at times throughout the 24 hours of each day so that you get ahead of the achey pain. Don't wait until you ache or it'll be hard to get on top of it. I made a chart and ticked off each dose/time, as I was completely useless at remembering if I'd taken pills or not. It was three ibuprofen and eight paracetamol in 24 hours. It was a bit tricky through the night to wake up and take them on time and find the biro to tick off the chart, but even if it went a bit skewiff during the night, the general rule of getting them down me early worked well. And remind yourself that it will get easier because for me and hopefully for you, the pain lifted towards the end of each three week cycle.

You will get more tired towards the end of the course, but just go with it and remember you will get stronger again.

Skin and hair

Towards the end of my treatment my complexion went really dry, red and scaly. It was awful and I looked much older. I gently applied olive oil each day, just pure olive oil out of the bottle and it was brilliant. I'm actually going to use it all the time from now on. It looks shiny at first but sinks in. If you put it on at bedtime it's all soaked up by morning. Of course you must drink plenty of water too. I am back to my usual complexion now, thank goodness, and I would say initially I got my designer stubble on my head (and down below!) about a month or so after the last infusion of drugs. It's really great when you see the shadow coming. My hair is more curly now with slightly more grey than before but I think it'll return to its usual condition eventually although I'm enjoying having a bit of a curl. I'm keeping it short too because I've had such nice compliments about cheekbones!

The most major drama was burning my face in the sun. I wasn't aware, although I should have guessed really, that after chemotherapy your skin burns really easily until all the cells have been replaced. You mustn't sit in the sun and make sure you slap on a high factor cream after your shower each morning. I bought some little tubes and put them in all my bags and pockets to make sure I was never without.

Genetics

I sent my details to the genetics department for information for my daughter on the likelihood of breast cancer being passed down to her. I asked at the very first appointment when my cancer was found and they gave me the forms to post then and there. After an appointment with the genetics specialist I was told that despite the fact that me, my mother and my grandmother had all had breast cancer, my daughter was still only moderate risk, a fact that I find hard to believe. This meant that I wouldn't be offered a gene test on the NHS and going privately was very expensive. I eventually signed up with The Breast and Ovarian Cancer Trials and was given the test for free. The test was to see if I had the BRCA 1 or 2 gene and fortunately it was negative. I have now offered more blood samples for genetic research into many genetic disorders. I thought it would be a way of paying the medical world back for their help because I would probably not have survived without them.

When you have an appointment with a consultant make sure you have questions written down. Make the most of their full attention because to see them later, after treatment has finished will be difficult and if you go privately, expensive. I could never think of questions during the appointments unless I had written them down ready to fire!

Radiotherapy

Radiotherapy has been very easy for me, but some of the lovely people that I've met in the waiting room have suffered more, it just depends what your cancer was and where the tumour was positioned I suppose.

I was given my radiotherapy treatment at a hospital about a forty minute drive away. Not all hospitals have the facilities so be prepared for a drive although apparently there is hospital transport if you ask for it. I quickly got used to the route and found it really easy compared to the chemotherapy.

On arrival each day I was shown through to the waiting room and then into the radiotherapy suite where I stripped off my top half of clothes and hopped onto the bed beneath the zappers. They gave me a little sheet to hold over my boobs for my modesty until the machine was ready. The staff were absolutely charming and always asked how I was and how I was recovering from the chemo. They then adjusted my position until they were satisfied with the measurements and went into their zapping room and set things off for about 30 seconds. This was painless. Apart from the noise you had no sensation at all. I had to go every day for eighteen days not including weekends. This is because they have to give you the treatment in small doses. The only side effect was a sore boob by about day ten which was healed nicely with daily applications of Aqueous cream, and I wasn't tired at all. Lots of people said I would be really tired but I drove myself and didn't have a problem with it at all. It must just depend how you are and what you've coped with before the treatment starts. Saying that,

I didn't push myself and made the drive the only thing I did all day. I suppose if you were trying to fit the appointments in whilst holding down a job and busy schedule elsewhere, you'd be bound to get really tired. I even took my husband sometimes and had pub lunches. Thought I may as well make a day of it!!

🍵 Health, diet and moving on …

Remember that as a nation we are prone to believe that cancer is 'The Big C' that everyone thinks is the end, but if you're aware of your body and speak up in time there is a good chance that you can survive breast cancer.

* * *

After your treatment you must decide how you want to move on with your life. I have met people who are happy to carry on eating unhealthy foods and drinking alcohol, as before, and that's up to them. I have vowed not to discuss my food and drink preferences unless people specifically want to because it can get so boring … but now, after finishing my chemo, I feel that its the only step I can take to contribute to survival. I am feeling really great considering what I've been through so I feel that my new healthy life style is surely helping me move on. I eat fresh foods and avoid *ready meals*, dairy and highly processed wheat. I am trying all sorts of healthy options with chickpeas and lentils, soya and coconut. There are an amazing number of alternatives when you look for them.

Many young people are creating a new style of cooking with fresh and raw ingredients. Look at Hemsley and Hemsley or Ella Woodward – great inspirations and the way forward for us all. Soup is fantastic if you get a hand blender and boil up any vegetables, not too long, just until tender, blitz and add lemon juice and seasoning. The Chinese noodle soups are easy to make and divine, add fresh coriander at the end. All the family will benefit. I am so proud of my daughter, she is a passionate cook creating beautiful healthy meals which will hold her in good stead for the future.

Eat well and don't be pasty and ill like vegetarians that don't eat vegetables. I've met them and they look awful. As soon as I was diagnosed with breast cancer I was scared to eat or drink anything unless it was organic fruit or vegetables. I suddenly understood people who were health freaks because I realised that when you have a health scare, the fear can take over your life. I didn't want to take the risk of not trying to be well because every day had become so precious, a gift.

I drink black tea and coffee alternating with herb tea and water through the day. One consultant said she recommended avoiding tea and coffee if you were prone to breast cysts as they were more common in coffee drinkers but there is no proof whatsoever that it is linked to cancer so I have the odd one now and then. Keeping herb tea in your handbag is a good idea for visiting because it's so annoying for people if you ask for something unusual.

Dairy

'Tea?' Auntie Sheila is filling the kettle at the sink,

'Ooh lovely, black please, I'm gasping.'

'Sorry?'

Sheila clicks the kettle on and shuffles over to me putting her hands on her hips with her eyebrows raised,

'No-one drinks black tea in Norfolk.'

'No milk or sugar.'

I forage around in my handbag looking for my herb tea bags as Sheila stares in horror.

'In fact can you pop one of these in a mug for me Sheila?' I continue, as I pass her a cranberry and cinnamon from my stash.

Auntie Sheila takes the tea bag from me as though it were

something dirty off my shoe and reluctantly drops it into a mug.

'Now Jane, pet, how do you expect to get through life without a decent cuppa, I mean this health malarkey is getting ridiculous if you don't mind me saying so. Your mother's told me all about this new … regime of yours.'

She steers me to an armchair and starts heaving my feet up onto her faux leather pouffe.

'Sit there, my girl, everyone needs a decent pot of Tetley after the M25.'

She carries on talking to me from the pantry,

'Just a dash of milk to take the roughness off.'

She re-appears with a tray of sandwiches.

'Auntie Sheila I told you I don't eat dairy anymore,' I said.

She shut her eyes,

'Don't panic!' she said, holding up a hand to reassure me.

'It's not dairy, just cheese and pickle.'

*   *   *

After my cancer ordeal I decided to stop eating dairy and beef. My breast care nurse and breast cancer specialist discouraged this decision because of the risk of osteoporosis. I was convinced by Jane Plants book about oestrogen in cows milk and the extra hormones injected into cows to boost milk production, organic or not, bearing in mind that my tumour was oestrogen fed. I replace my calcium intake with almonds, sardines, apricots, dark greens and tahini paste. Having to explain this to people can be tedious, but they seem very keen to discuss it. You have to do what's right for you. Visiting seems to be the only tricky time for non-dairy eating. When I'm at home I don't even think about it. There is butter and cream in so many foods especially ready meals and you have to accept that you will have to enjoy a fruit sorbet while everybody else gets stuck into an ice cream. Always ask for non-dairy items in restaurants and cafes because this will promote it and hopefully expand the choices on menus eventually. You must talk to your doctor and a nutritional expert to discuss a good diet plan in case you have other health issues which would be affected by a non-dairy diet. Apparently breast cancer was very rare in the Far East where they didn't consume cow milk until recent years. Now that they are changing to a more western diet, breast cancer cases are slowly rising. Dairy obviously means cheese, cream, butter, milk chocolate and all the lovely things, but I am slimmer now and full of energy so I feel I am reaping the benefits. Butter is in cake ... I know right? ... quite a challenge, but there are amazing recipes with dark chocolate, dates, honey and coconut oil. Ella Woodward is an inspiration for people trying to avoid dairy, but who like to stuff their faces with cake every now and then ... I think that's most women.

The good news is that if you give up sugar you will find your palate changes and you don't crave sweet things after a few months.

*   *   *

The other day my friend's mother was nibbling a corner of a cucumber sandwich and lecturing us all on diet and well-being.

'Well of course giving up dairy completely is ridiculous, Jane. It should be everything in moderation.'

We are all nodding politely as we sit in her beautiful sunny garden. A year ago I would have been secretly wishing that I could carry the plate of jam and cream scones from the table to a quiet corner of her garden and eat them all in peace. I have never been able to do anything at all in moderation and the phrase depresses me. If something is nice then I want as much of it as I can get. I think that most of my true friends feel the same way. Unfortunately, being dairy free triggers off long discussions on diet wherever you go. However, this yearning for dairy-laden heaven has subsided over the last year and I am now quite surprised how my food preferences have changed. I have been known to eat a whole bag of walnuts and four bananas instead of a bar of chocolate, but apparently that won't cause any damage.

Booze and socialising again

The last few chords of 'Don't Stop Me Now' by Queen ricochet across the lounge and I roll over on the floor where I can see a row of high-heeled feet along the foot of the sofa. I pull myself up to standing, gasping for breath and sweating profusely from my performance as I take a bow to the rapturous applause of my friends.

It's time to go home, though, and I'm exhausted so I make my way to the hall, looking for my shoes.

'Oh my God someone get Jane a taxi,' slurs my dear friend, Sarah, as she fills her glass and comes into the hallway.

I throw on my jacket and head for the door.

'I'm fine, darling, I've got the car actually. Do you want a lift?'

The evening has been a perfect example of how I don't miss booze or need a drink in order to have a good time.

Giving up booze has been so easy. There is funny, lovely drunk and there is awful, ugly drunk. I don't miss the latter and find that I can reach funny, lovely drunk on sparkling water if I'm with good company. I have laughed hysterically just as often over a cup of tea as I have drinking Pinot Grigio and I certainly don't miss the hangovers. Of course there is also the money saving side of things as well. Taxis and wine are expensive.

Following the recommendation from my surgeon I have given up alcohol and it is really easy. I feel wonderful so it was obviously dragging me down. People do make a face when I ask for sparkling water, but the difference now is that I don't care if they have a problem with it. I can hit them with my rather reasonable excuse. The surgeon said that statistically I have a 10% higher chance of a cancer recurrence if I drink …, say no more.

After hiding up throughout my chemo I really missed socialising. The joy of seeing people again was immense when the treatment was over. On the day of my last chemo infusion the girl next to me was sent home because her temperature was slightly up and she had to add another week onto the long treatment plan. She was devastated. This confirmed that isolation **will** keep you on course and avoid delays from picking up colds, etc. It was really hard to console friends and family who found this hard, but you can't afford to weaken for them. **You** are the one coping with the treatment and they must try to understand. Phone calls and Skype make it much easier.

*   *   *

When the last chemo dose had gone in I started to think about going on walks with friends. Then after a month I really enjoyed going to houses, restaurants, theatre, public transport, etc. to see my treasured chums.

*   *   *

Don't over do it though because you will get tired quickly for a while. Set yourself little goals, maybe a list of smallish jobs and choose one or two for each day so you feel you're getting something done. Don't be disappointed if you are tired, it's inevitable that you will be for quite a while after the marathon you've been through, some people more than others, it depends what drugs they gave you and what sort of cancer you had. Give your body a chance to get strong again. You'll have good and bad days. I found it best to force myself to get up in the morning and do something and then I usually felt better. You can always hop back to bed if you're really struggling. I exercised gently to regain my strength with yoga and walks around the garden. I had really weak legs towards the end of my treatment so I started with gentle daily walks incorporating a bit of a jog eventually. At the end of chemo I had tired muscles especially in my thighs. I started going for a daily march around a field to get the blood pumping round and it really helped, as did yoga, but there were a few weeks when it was hard to even get up the stairs. Don't panic because your strength **will** return.

My main aim of exercising is to help my lymphatic system work. After you have had lymph nodes removed you may have a feeling of swelling on the affected armpit and possibly in the breast. There is no cure for this apart from getting the blood pumping round your body with walks and swims. I find this keeps it at bay and I've got used to the sensation and it doesn't bother me nearly as much as it did at first. The blood is pumped by the heart but the lymphatic system has no pump so struggles to drain the affected side with less nodes, but the exercise must get it moving around surely?

*   *   *

I swim every other day for an hour if I can. It takes a lot of discipline and a nice local swimming pool to tempt me, but I miss it if I don't go now. I just do gentle swimming, not thrashing up and down like a maniac. I go to pilates and yoga and I walk a lot too. I avoid taking the car at every opportunity and leave earlier. Obviously this is easier in the spring and summer when it's pleasant weather and also when you don't have a job and children to worry about. Whatever your situation, if you can incorporate some time for yourself into your week as much as you can then you will be healthier and happier. Stress is bad …

*   *   *

Here is an example of how we are prone to unconsciously living stressful lives. Mums are particularly vulnerable.

My friend Samantha was recovering from her breast lumpectomy after a diagnosis of breast cancer and the nurse had advised that she aim to make some changes to her life style and avoid stress. A few months had passed and the family were relaxed and reassured that she was going to be alright so things had generally gone back to normal at home. Samantha booked a wonderful day of therapy treatments to boost her confidence and well-being only to realise that it was on the day that her twenty year old daughter needed a lift to the airport on her way to stay for a holiday with Samantha's sister in Paris. She decided that this was a typical example of where she needed to make some changes in family life and allow time for herself. She could drop her daughter off at the airport and drive straight to the spa for her relaxing day instead of cancelling the whole thing.

After waving off her daughter at the airport Samantha sheepishly switched off her mobile phone. This was not something that she was used to doing and it felt wrong, but she set off for what was a blissful afternoon of swimming, yoga and massage.

Before she drove home Samantha sat in her car feeling rested. With beautiful classical music playing and looking out at the view of the garden at the spa, she switched her phone back on and within seconds it was leaping and buzzing on the passengers seat.

There were many voicemails.

Husband: 'Samantha where are you? for f***s sake switch your f****** phone on. Your daughter is stranded in Paris because your idiot sister has failed to meet her at the airport.'

Daughter: 'Mum!! Fiona isn't here … Mum?'

Husband: 'Sam, I can't believe this, call me NOW!'

Daughter: 'Mum I've found a cafe and I'll try ringing Auntie Fiona.'

Husband: 'I can't get hold of anyone! AAAGH!'

Daughter: 'Hi Mum, I found Auntie Fiona and we're at the Eiffel Tower. It's amazing.'

Husband: 'Just to let you know Chloe is fine, if you ever get this, I mean don't feel bad or anything.'

* * *

A few days into Chloe's Paris trip Samantha was at my house having a cup of tea and worrying that she hadn't heard from her. Later on her phone rang.

'Darling! Oh at last! How are you, are you OK, is everything alright? You fell over! Oh no have you broken anything? What? Oh you're HUNG over!'

We laughed so much and reassured ourselves that we had to stop worrying about our children and that they were quite capable now and had to experience life standing on their own two feet without having to report back to us every moment.

Menopause and chemotherapy

'Let's light a fire, darling!'

I wiggle my non-existent eyebrows and flutter my bald eyelids seductively as I wipe my red nose that has been dripping since lunch-time. I'm freezing and the central heating is on full pelt. I replace my sunglasses which have been helping my eyes not to water as I snuggle down under a blanket on the sofa. It's the height of summer.

Poor Steve goes to the trouble of chopping logs and cleaning the hearth only to come back to the kitchen where I have stripped off all my jumpers and opened the back door.

'Oh my God it's so hot in this house!'

I'm fanning myself with the Gazette and yanking my socks off.

'I think I'll just sit in the garden and paint my nails,' I mutter, stepping out onto the terrace in my pants.

Welcome to the Menopause.

Steve stops in his tracks and calmly places the log basket by the wood burner and goes off in search of red nail varnish. At the end of my treatment all my nails started to peel away from the nail bed and went black. I didn't panic because I'd been warned that it might happen and I painted them red immediately. This worked fine and I trimmed them often so that I avoided catching them on things ... after a while you can see the new lovely pink nail that has grown half way so I'm feeling good about that. The nurse told me to wear gloves for housework, etc. to avoid infection underneath. About six months after my chemo I noticed that my toe nails were weak and black in places, too, so I suppose it was the chemo working its way through. Get the red varnish out again.

*　　*　　*

I get hot flushes now that I am on Tamoxifen and going through the menopause which was brought on by the chemotherapy. My periods stopped immediately with chemotherapy which wasn't that much of a problem for a fifty year old. They used to be heavy and every three weeks where I felt that I was heaving with hormones so that could be, for me, one of the good things to come from chemo. I don't have any aroma from my armpits now so it must be the oestrogen that smells which is stopped by the Tamoxifen!

When you start to go out socialising again make sure you wear several layers right down to a strappy top so that you can stabilise your temperature as it goes up and down all evening. You'll probably annoy everyone in the theatre as you remove and replace your cardigan throughout the evening but that's tough, at least you're out!

Moving on

I still have decisions to make about moving on. My surgeon convinced me that I don't need mastectomies and I am starting to relax more. Since my chemo and now that I am taking Tamoxifen, the oestrogen blocker, I have found that the cysts have stopped forming so I'm not constantly worrying that I have another lump.

As far as general day-to-day moving on, you may want to decide not to talk about it. I say this because I am just back from a walk in the town and some people, when they know you've had a cancer scare, assume you're going to die and look really surprised to see you! This emphasises my point that we need to educate ourselves about the different types of cancer and the great recovery rate for breast cancer. We only hear the sad stuff and see the awful fund-raising ads on TV that paint such a bleak picture so no wonder some people grab your hand and say things like,

'Oh my God, fingers crossed, take care,'

They may as well say,

'It was nice knowing you!'

You will also find that they want to tell you all about all the other people they know that had cancer … there are people dying every day from all sorts of things and all we can do is try to be sensible and keep it in perspective. Keep in touch with your body, how it works, what it needs and work at it. It will work for you if you look after it. Get to the doctor if you're worried about something that has changed slightly or a new pain.

One year on

It was a year ago that I had my lump removed and now I am supposed to get on with my life and put the whole experience behind me. Life carries on with its events and dramas, which tend to take your mind off your boob worries. However, I still feel about for lumps every day, several times. My husband suggested that perhaps I stopped doing it in restaurants. I have had visits to the hospital to show them areas of my boob that seem suspicious and they try hard to convince me after an ultrasound investigation that I mustn't let my life pass me by while I worry it away. They don't want to offer me a double mastectomy so I have to be brave and just keep a close eye on things or alternatively, get it done privately. Since I started my new diet of healthiness, yoga and swimming I have very small boobs. I hope this will mean that if any more cancerous lumps grow, I will be more likely to notice them and get them scanned. The genetics consultant was so kind and reassured me that with close surveillance, even if I did have a recurrence, it would now be spotted immediately and they could nip it out straight away.

It's been a tough year, but I am luckier than many. I have seen grief and loss in other families, some cancer related and some tragic accidents that have turned their world upside down. I now realise that we must treasure each day and be thankful for what we have.

Do stuff.

 **Glossary**

I found that one of the best sources of information was the MacMillan Cancer Support website:

www.macmillan.org.uk

with some additional useful advice found on the Cancer Research UK website:

www.cancerresearchuk.org

Another useful site is the American National Breast Cancer Foundation:

www.nationalbreastcancer.org

For UK people the contacts and other information on this latter US-based organisation are not so useful but the text information is still perfectly valid and well explained. For ease, to give a quick overview and especially for those who do not regularly use the internet, below is a glossary of terms that you may hear and wonder what they mean. It is not an exhaustive list and you should ask your doctor to explain things if you do not understand.

Biopsy

This is a medical procedure. A small sample of tissue is taken from your lump and examined under a microscope by a pathologist. Medically I think that this process is called histopathology. The tests determine whether the lump is malignant (dangerous) or benign (not harmful). My biopsy was not painful. The ultrasound lady numbed the area and I felt nothing. It was a bit bruised a day or so later, that's all.

Breast Cancer Gene

Genes are the building blocks of each of the cells within our body. Genes are how characteristics are passed from one generation to another. A gene is made up of DNA (DeoxyriboNucleic Acids) and other groups of acids that contain information about us which can then be passed on to our offspring. With the incidence of breast cancer in women growing, many people are concerned that this is due to heredity aspects passed on through these genes. Currently in the UK about one in every nine people will develop breast cancer at some time in their lives, but since we still do no know enough about the causes of cancer, let alone breast cancer, it seems churlish to blame this all on to our genes. For the most part the influence of diet and other factors may play an even stronger role. However, scientists have found that a fault in some genes is linked to a higher risk of breast cancer. The most commonly discussed of these genes are the BRCA 1 and BRCA 2 genes (usually pronounced BRACA). A fault in these genes not only increases the risk of breast cancer but also the risk to develop ovarian cancer. If there is a strong family history of breast cancer in the UK, the NHS offer genetic testing to establish if this fault is present by using a simple analysis of a sample of blood. However, in my case, despite my mother and grandmother both having had breast cancer, my case was only considered as 'moderate' since their cancers did not appear until they were in their 60s. Private testing is of course possible and the cost of these will surely come down in the next few years plus the ability to analyse more of the genes that may lead to cancer – so don't give up hope.

Cancer

Cancer is a condition where the DNA of a cell is damaged or altered so that the cell grows abnormally. A collection of cancer cells form a tumour.

Cancer and Dairy

Jane Plant is the author of a book that promotes a dairy free (and reduced animal protein) diet to reduce/prevent breast cancer (Your Life in Your Hands, Virgin Books 2007). As a research scientist when she herself had breast cancer she looked at studies of the number of breast cancer sufferers among Chinese women. These studies found the incidence to be significantly lower for Chinese women compared to women in the West, also noting that for Chinese women who had lived in the West and consumed a Western diet, the rate increased to be more in line with other Western women. Her conjecture is that the increased incidence is due to diet. One of the cited reasons is that milk contains hormones that are now strongly linked to the development of some cancers. While there is good scientific evidence put forward by Professor Plant (an Emeritus professor of Earth Sciences at Imperial College) Cancer Research UK says that the results currently do not give any clear evidence. Indeed there are many good reasons why dairy is good for us, and when I had a second opinion about the pros and cons of chemotherapy my consultant suggested that I did not give up dairy and so it is not a clear cut decision.

Carcinoma

A carcinoma is a form of tumour which forms when a person has cancer. The name is used for the growth or group of cells that produce a lump when the cancer begins in the skin or tissues surrounding organs.

Chemotherapy

Chemotherapy, or chemo, is the term used for the treatment

where anti-cancer drugs are used either to cure a patient of cancer or given to reduce symptoms where a cure is not possible (this latter treatment would then be called palliative care). The drugs are released slowly into the body via a drip attached to a thin tube called a cannula. Since you have to sit for a couple of hours while this takes place, the cannula is, where possible, placed in the back of the hand or in the crook of your arm below your bicep (sometimes called a PICC line, standing for Peripherally Inserted Central Catheter). If the veins in your arm do not cooperate then the drugs can be administered via a tube in your chest or neck (called a Hickman line, or just Hick line, named after the person who first pioneered its use). There may be other medical reasons why a Hick line is preferred. One reason is that a Hick line may be left in between treatments. In my case the chemo started about twelve weeks after my surgery so I had time to recover from the surgery before the chemo started.

CT Scan

A CT scan, or CAT scan, is a specialised X-Ray which provides information about the soft tissues within the body which do not show up on normal X-Rays. The letters stand for Computerised Tomography, where the tomography bit refers to sections that build up to form a three dimensional image.

Doctor/ Registrar/Consultant

Your local, or community doctor is a GP, or General Practitioner. They are a medical doctor and have completed a five-year university degree followed by several years of training. Oddly enough they do not usually hold a doctorate degree (which is historically called a Ph.D., or Doctor of Philosophy, taken by many research scientists). A Registrar is a middle-ranking hospital doctor undergoing specialist training towards becoming a specialist. A consultant is someone who has finished all their training and is a specialist in their field, has qualifications as a specialist and has taken up a post as a specialist in a hospital. A surgeon is a person who performs surgery. Surgeons are also consultants.

Ductal carcinoma in situ

When the cancer first forms it may remain within the breast ducts and is then said to be in situ (it's Latin for locally).

FEC-T

FEC-T is a chemotherapy treatment commonly used for the treatment of breast cancer which is a combination of drugs. The first three letters stand for the drugs

> F = Fluorouracil
>
> E = Epirubicin
>
> C = Cyclophosphamide

which are given together usually over three visits, each three weeks apart. Each visit takes about 2-3 hours. They first attach a line to your vein and flush it through with some saline water to hydrate your veins (and open then up), then the drugs are slowly administered, and this is followed by a further saline to flush the drugs through. Then, later the drug

> T = Taxotere (also known as Docetaxel)

is given for the second half of the treatment, again over three similar sittings.

Grade

Cancers are graded according to how quickly they are growing. This can only be determined after a biopsy or a lumpectomy to analyse the cancerous cells. A pathology report grades invasive cancer into one of three grades:

- Grade 1 - cancer cells are similar size and shape to normal cells and are usually slow growing.
- Grade 2 - the cancer cells are a bit different to normal cells and the cancer is faster growing.
- Grade 3 - the cancer cells are clearly different from normal cells and the cancer is fast-growing.

For cancer described as ductal carcinoma, the grading is more or less the same but sometimes the terms low, intermediate or high are used instead of 1, 2 and 3.

Herceptin

Herceptin is the brand name for a drug commonly used in breast cancer treatment for those who are HER2 positive, meaning that they have high levels of a growth factor which tends to mean that the cancer grows faster (the HER stands for Human Epidermal Receptor). When you have the lump removed they test for HER2. In my case I was not HER2 positive.

Hormone receptors

In cell biology, a receptor is a cell, or part of a cell, that responds to a particular stimulus. In breast cancer, this usually comes up when the pathology report on some of your cancer cells determines whether they are receptive to oestrogen or not. If the cancer cells have receptors for oestrogen they are referred to as OestrogenReceptor+ (but in the international literature sometimes abbreviated to ER+ because in the USA they drop the 'o' and spell it estrogen). Then, just like normal breast cells, the growth of cancer cells is promoted by the presence of oestrogen. If this is the case, then the treatment available after surgery to reduce the risk of spreading is with hormone therapy treatments such as Tamoxifen. Tamoxifen blocks the oestrogen from reaching any cancer cells so that they either grow only slowly or they do not grow at all. As with all current breast cancer treatments, there is so much research on-going that even within a few years things will probably have changed, but the current advice is that Tamoxifen is given to breast cancer sufferers who are ER+ for at least 10 years and potentially more.

Invasive Cancer
Invasive ductal cancer is the most common type of breast cancer and is where the cancer has spread outside the breast ducts to the surrounding tissue and can therefore potentially spread to other parts of the body.

Lumpectomy
A lumpectomy is the surgical procedure to remove a cancerous 'lump' from the breast.

Lymph nodes and lymphedema
In our bodies a network of lymph nodes (pronounced limf) form a lymphatic system which collects fluid that forms outside the system of blood vessels. The fluid (that is the lymph bit) is a

clear watery fluid which also includes some waste material. You have lymph nodes in your chest, armpit, neck, groin and other places around the body and the system collects the fluid, with it eventually being passed into a blood vessel near your heart.

Following my surgery to remove the lump, traces of cancer were also found in my sentinel lymph node, meaning that the cancer had begun to spread. To further check to see how far it had spread, 17 other lymph nodes were removed which, in my case, were found to be clear. After surgery, this meant that lymph fluid would collect under my arm and so a drain was initially put in to relieve the pressure. Apparently the body should eventually learn to live without these nodes and the fluid will disperse.

Lymphedema is a reasonably common side effect of surgery following breast cancer and radiotherapy whereby excessive fluid builds up (that is the edema bit). There are massage treatments to improve the condition. In my case I have swelling under my arm and I am trying to manage this with gentle exercise like yoga and swimming plus a bit of massage.

Mammogram

A mammogram, or mammograph, is an X-Ray of the breast which uses a low energy radiation as a diagnostic screening to identify early traces of breast cancer. Each breast in turn is placed between flat plates. Some people find it uncomfortable. The picture, or film, is 'read' by a radiologist or a radiographer.

Mastectomy

A mastectomy is the surgical procedure to remove the entire breast tissue.

Oncologist

The term oncologist means the doctor who specialises in the treatment of cancer. In my case I had three different types; the surgical oncologist who cut out the lump; the medical oncologist, who oversaw my chemotherapy; and another one that oversaw my radiotherapy. These people work together.

Radiotherapy

Radiotherapy is a localised treatment for breast cancer. It uses high-energy radiation to kill any cancer cells that remain after surgery. For me the process started with three dots being tattooed on my chest, one in the middle and one either side, so that for each visit, the precise location of my cancer could be targetted. They cannot give you one big treatment of radiotherapy, it has to be given in lots of small doses. Because of this you have to travel to the hospital every day for three weeks. Most people find the daily travel harder than the treatment itself.

Remission

Luckily this word has not been used for me. Remission is usually used when you have had cancer, it's been treated and, although perhaps still lurking, is not currently showing any outward signs. In other words the medical people are not sure if or when it will return. In my case I like to think of myself as being cured.

Sentinel node

In everyday parlance, the word sentinel is usually used for the soldier who watches out, or guards over an army. The sentinel guard places themselves in a prominent position and is supposed to be there to raise the alarm if there is any danger. In cancer terms the sentinel node is thus the first node that lymph fluid reaches from a cancerous tumour. In my treatment, a dye was inserted near to my cancer via an injection and its path was tracked to identify the sentinel node. Sadly, in our lymph system the sentinel node does not raise the alarm though unless you have a biopsy - that is why we need to self check ourselves for growths.

Size

The size of a breast cancer is the measurement of the 'lump' measured in millimetres (mm) or centimetres (cm). But it is not only size that matters, it is also important to know how fast a cancer is growing.

Stage

This is a bit tricky to explain. The stage measures how far the cancer has grown, or spread but includes information on the size. Basically it tries to say something about how three things are varying with just a single measure. A bit like saying whether your car engine is in a healthy state by just looking at the temperature gauge.

The stage of a cancer depends on three things:

- the size of the lump
- whether the cancer cells have spread to the lymph nodes
- whether the cancer has spread to other parts of the body (if it has, they say that the cancer has metastasised. A secondary cancer is called a metastasised cancer)

There are commonly four stages but it gets rather confusing since there are several combinations. You should ask your doctor for a detailed description but basically:

- Stage 1 - the lump is small, less than 2 cm. This can be split into two sub parts. The first, 1A is where the cancer has not spread to the lymph nodes, while 1B is where there is evidence of cancer cells in the lymph nodes.
- Stage 2 - typically the lump is bigger than 2 cm but not bigger than 5 cm. Again there may be a subdivision to distinguish whether the lymph nodes are affected or not.
- Stage 3 - variations exist but generally this is where the lump is bigger than 5 cm or it has spread to several lymph nodes.
- Stage 4 - is where the cancer has spread to other parts of the body (metastasised).

The Cancer Research UK site has some diagrams that explain this better in a simpler, pictoral form than the text above. See

http://www.cancerresearchuk.org/about-cancer/type/breast-cancer/treatment/number-stages-of-breast-cancer

as does the National Breast Cancer Foundation, see

http://www.nationalbreastcancer.org/breast-cancer-stages

Steroids

Steroids are prescribed by the oncologist to be taken just before your chemotherapy treatments and for two days afterwards. These are generally in tablet form and are usually given to reduce sickness or other side effects of the chemo. They have different names, such as Dexamethasone. Before the nurse starts the chemo she always asks if you have taken the steroid – I always did, fearing that the treatment would not go ahead if I had missed a tablet.

During your chemo treatment you may also require an immune booster to be administered via an injection. In my case via a self-administered injection into the spare tyre around my tummy. Don't worry, the needle was really thin and I hardly noticed it going in. In my case, the syringe had a clever spring mechanism so that the needle retracted inside the syringe once the shot had been administered. It was a new experience and I reminded myself that some people, some of them children, have to do that every day to control other conditions, so I couldn't make a fuss.

Tamoxifen

Tamoxifen is a commonly used treatment for breast cancer sufferers post surgery. It is a form of hormone therapy blocking the path of oestrogen to the cancer cells to prevent re-occurrence.

About the Author

Jane Hoggar grew up in Suffolk. On finishing school she danced and sang her way around the world for six years before settling in Hertfordshire where she has lived for twenty-four years with her husband and children.

Her career has covered many areas including:
Glamorous Showgirl Extraordinaire (that was the abroad bit)
Singer
Dance and drama teacher
Magician's Assistant
Kitchen Assistant
Shop Assistant
Classroom Assistant
Dinner Lady
Receptionist
Bed and Breakfast Land lady
Mum (She was being a Mum throughout all these jobs, except the first one of course)

She's not idle, always planning her next business enterprise.